Modern Critical Interpretations

Joseph Conrad's
Lord Jim

Modern Critical Interpretations

These and other titles in preparation

Modern Critical Interpretations

Joseph Conrad's
Lord Jim

.

Edited and with an introduction by

Harold Bloom
Sterling Professor of the Humanities
Yale University

Chelsea House Publishers ◊ *1987*
NEW YORK ◊ NEW HAVEN ◊ PHILADELPHIA

© 1987 by Chelsea House Publishers,
a division of Chelsea House Educational Communications, Inc.,
  95 Madison Avenue, New York, NY 10016
  345 Whitney Avenue, New Haven, CT 06511
  5014 West Chester Pike, Edgemont, PA 19028

Introduction © 1987 by Harold Bloom

Printed and bound in the United States of America

∞ The paper used in this publication meets the minimum
requirements of the American National Standard for
Permanence of Paper for Printed Library Materials,
Z39.48–1984.

Library of Congress Cataloging-in-Publication Data
Joseph Conrad's Lord Jim
    (Modern critical interpretations)
    Bibliography: p.
    Includes index.
    1. Conrad, Joseph, 1857–1924. Lord Jim.
I. Bloom, Harold. II. Series.
PR6005.04L7344   1987   823'.912   86-33460
ISBN 1-55546-016-X (alk. paper)

Contents

Editor's Note

This book brings together a representative selection of the best criticism available upon Joseph Conrad's novel *Lord Jim*. The critical essays are reprinted here in the chronological order of their original publication. I am grateful to Guy Moppel for his aid in editing this volume.

My introduction contemplates first the enigma of Conrad as an impressionistic storyteller, and then goes on to consider some of the enigmas of Marlow's portrayal of Jim. Elliott B. Gose, Jr. begins the chronological sequence of criticism with a defense of Jim's right, as a dreamer, to have lived and died as a dreamer. The focus shifts to Conrad himself in Peter J. Glassman's account of how *Lord Jim* embodies "Conrad's will to identify and to justify himself."

In a brief but useful note, D. M. Halperin relates Jim's "leap" into cowardice to St. Augustine's celebrated "Pear Tree Caper." Ian Watt, Conrad's most definitive critic (in my judgment), broods on the ending of the novel and tries to determine whether it can be judged to be "tragic." The ending is also a concern of Suresh Raval's examination of "Conrad's art of failure," which is found to ensue in such tensions between language and self that the book's conclusion has to be elusive and contradictory.

J. Hillis Miller, our finest living critic in the deconstructive mode of Derrida and the late Paul de Man, gives us a *Lord Jim* whose meanings are multiform and undecidable, involved as they are in the metaphoric repetitions of language itself. This volume ends with Daniel Cottom's more politicized reading, in which poor Jim is seen as "the very image of Western imperialism in the modern world"—obsessed, rhetorically empty, pridefully suicidal.

Introduction

In Conrad's "Youth" (1898), Marlow gives us a brilliant description of the sinking of the *Judea:*

> "Between the darkness of earth and heaven she was burning fiercely upon a disc of purple sea shot by the blood-red play of gleams; upon a disc of water glittering and sinister. A high, clear flame, an immense and lonely flame, ascended from the ocean, and from its summit the black smoke poured continuously at the sky. She burned furiously; mournful and imposing like a funeral pile kindled in the night, surrounded by the sea, watched over by the stars. A magnificent death had come like a grace, like a gift, like a reward to that old ship at the end of her laborious day. The surrender of her weary ghost to the keeper of stars and sea was stirring like the sight of a glorious triumph. The masts fell just before daybreak, and for a moment there was a burst and turmoil of sparks that seemed to fill with flying fire the night patient and watchful, the vast night lying silent upon the sea. At daylight she was only a charred shell, floating still under a cloud of smoke and bearing a glowing mass of coal within.
>
> "Then the oars were got out, and the boats forming in a line moved round her remains as if in procession—the longboat leading. As we pulled across her stern a slim dart of fire shot out viciously at us, and suddenly she went down, head first, in a great hiss of steam. The unconsumed stern was the last to sink; but the paint had gone, had cracked, had peeled off, and there were no letters, there was no word, no stubborn device that was like her soul, to flash at the rising sun her creed and her name."

The apocalyptic vividness is enhanced by the visual nameless-
ness of the "unconsumed stern," as though the creed of Christ's
people maintained both its traditional refusal to violate the Second
Commandment, and its traditional affirmation of its not-to-be-
named God. With the *Judea,* Conrad sinks the romance of youth's
illusions, but like all losses in Conrad this submersion in the destructive element is curiously dialectical, since only experiential loss al-
lows for the compensation of an imaginative gain in the representation
of artistic truth. Originally the ephebe of Flaubert and of Flaubert's
"son," Maupassant, Conrad was reborn as the narrative disciple of
Henry James, the James of *The Spoils of Poynton* and *What Maisie
Knew* rather than the James of the final phase.

Ian Watt convincingly traces the genesis of Marlow to the way
that "James developed the indirect narrative approach through the
sensitive central intelligence of one of the characters." Marlow, whom
James derided as "that preposterous magic mariner," actually represents Conrad's swerve away from the excessive strength of James's
influence upon him. By always "mixing himself up with the narrative," in James's words, Marlow guarantees an enigmatic reserve
that increases the distance between the impressionistic techniques of
Conrad and James. Though there is little valid comparison that can
be made between Conrad's greatest achievements and the hesitant,
barely fictional status of Pater's *Marius the Epicurean,* Conrad's impressionism is as extreme and solipsistic as Pater's. There is a definite
parallel between the fates of Sebastian Van Storck (in Pater's *Imaginary Portraits*) and Decoud in *Nostromo.*

In his 1897 preface to *The Nigger of the "Narcissus,"* Conrad
famously insisted that his creative task was "before all to make you
see." He presumably was aware that he thus joined himself to a line
of prose seers whose latest representatives were Carlyle, Ruskin, and
Pater. There is a movement in that group from Carlyle's exuberant
"Natural Supernaturalism" through Ruskin's paganization of Evan-
gelical fervor to Pater's evasive and skeptical Epicurean materialism,
with its eloquent suggestion that all we can see is the flux of sensations. Conrad exceeds Pater in the reduction of impressionism to a
state of consciousness where the seeing narrator is hopelessly mixed
up with the seen narrative. James may seem an impressionist when
compared to Flaubert, but alongside of Conrad he is clearly shown to
be a kind of Platonist, imposing forms and resolutions upon the flux
of human relations by an exquisite formal geometry altogether his
own.

To observe that Conrad is metaphysically less of an Idealist is hardly to argue that he is necessarily a stronger novelist than his master, James. It may suggest though that Conrad's originality is more disturbing than that of James, and may help explain why Conrad, rather than James, became the dominant influence upon the generation of American novelists that included Hemingway, Fitzgerald, and Faulkner. The cosmos of *The Sun Also Rises*, *The Great Gatsby*, and *As I Lay Dying* derives from *Heart of Darkness* and *Nostromo* rather than from *The Ambassadors* and *The Golden Bowl*. Darl Bundren is the extreme inheritor of Conrad's quest to carry impressionism into its heart of darkness in the human awareness that we are only a flux of sensations gazing outwards upon a flux of impressions.

II

Lord Jim (1900) is the first of Conrad's five great novels, followed by what seems to me the finest, *Nostromo* (1904), and then by the marvelous sequence of *The Secret Agent* (1906), *Under Western Eyes* (1910), and finally *Victory* (1914). Of these, it seems clear that *Lord Jim* has the closest to universal appeal; I have rarely met a reader who was not fascinated by it. Martin Price, the subtlest of Conrad's moral critics, prefers *Lord Jim* to *Nostromo* because he finds that both the author's skepticism and the author's romanticism are given their full scope in *Lord Jim* rather than in *Nostromo*. Doubtless this is true, but Jim himself lacks the high romantic appeal of the magnificent Nostromo, and I prefer also the corrosive skepticism of Decoud to the skeptical wisdom of Marlow and Stein. Not that I would deprecate *Lord Jim*; had Conrad written nothing else, this single novel would have guaranteed his literary survival.

Aaron Fogel, writing on *Nostromo*, sees it as marking Conrad's transition from an Oedipal emphasis (as in *Lord Jim*) to a representation of the self's struggle against more outward influences. Certainly Jim's struggle does suit Fogel's formulation of the earlier mode in Conrad: "the denial, by internalization, of the Oedipal order of forced dialogue in the outside world—the translation of inquisition into an inner feeling of compulsion to quarrel with a forebear or with oneself." Though there is much of Conrad in Marlow, and a little of him in Stein, his true surrogate is surely Jim, whose dialectics of defeat are in some sense a late version of Polish romanticism, of the perpetual defeat of Polish heroism. This is only to intimate that Jim's

Byronism is rather more Polish than British. Jim rarely demands anything, and he never demands victory. One way of understanding the novel is to see how incomprehensible it would be if Conrad had chosen to make his hero an American.

Marlow, our narrator, becomes something like a father to Jim, in an implicit movement that has been shrewdly traced by Ian Watt. There is an impressive irony in the clear contrast between the eloquent father, Marlow, and the painfully inarticulate son, Jim. The relation between the two poignantly enhances our sense of just how vulnerable Jim is and cannot cease to be. Marlow is a survivor, capable of withstanding nearly the full range of human experience, while Jim is doom-eager, as much a victim of the romantic imagination as he is a belated instance of its intense appeal to us.

Albert J. Guerard associated *Lord Jim* with *Absalom, Absalom!* (a not un-Conradian work) as novels that become different with each attentive reading. Jim's "simplicity" takes the place of the charismatic quality we expect of the romantic protagonist, and Guerard sees Jim as marked by a conflict between personality and will. But Jim's personality remains a mystery to us, almost despite Marlow, and Jim's will is rarely operative, so far as I can see. What we can know about Jim is the enormous strength and prevalence of his fantasy-making powers, which we need not confuse with a romantic imagination, since *that* hardly excludes self-knowledge. Indeed, the deepest puzzle of Jim is why should he fascinate anyone at all, let alone Marlow, Stein, Conrad, and ourselves? Why is he endless to meditation?

Everyone who has read *Lord Jim* (and many who have not) remember its most famous statement, which is Stein's:

> A man that is born falls into a dream like a man who falls into the sea. If he tries to climb out into the air as inexperienced people endeavour to do, he drowns—*nicht wahr?* . . . No! I tell you! The way is to the destructive element submit yourself, and with the exertions of your hands and feet in the water make the deep, deep sea keep you up.

That describes Stein's romanticism, but hardly Jim's, since Jim cannot swim in the dream-world. When he seems to make the destructive element keep him up, as in Patusan, there would always have to be a Gentleman Brown waiting for him. An imagination like

Jim's, which has little sense of otherness, falls into identification as the truly destructive element, and the error of identifying with the outrageous Brown is what kills Jim. Tony Tanner deftly compares Brown to Iago, if only because Brown's hatred for Jim approximates Iago's hatred for Othello, but Brown has a kind of rough justice in denying Jim's moral superiority. That returns us to the enigma of Jim: why does he make such a difference for Marlow—and for us?

We know the difference between Jim and Brown, even if Jim cannot, even as we know that Jim never will mature into Stein. Is Jim merely the spirit of illusion, or does there linger in him something of the legitimate spirit of romance? Marlow cannot answer the question, and we cannot either, no matter how often we read *Lord Jim*. Is that a strength or a weakness in this novel? That Conrad falls into obscurantism, particularly in *Heart of Darkness,* is beyond denial. Is *Lord Jim* simply an instance of such obscurantism on a larger scale?

Impressionist fiction necessarily forsakes the Idealist metaphysics of the earlier romantic novel, a metaphysics that culminated in George Eliot. Marlow beholding Jim is a concourse of sensations recording a flood of impressions; how can a sensation distinguish whether an impression is authentic or not? Yet Marlow is haunted by the image of heroism, and finds an authentic realization of the image in Stein. The famous close of Marlow's narrative invokes Jim as an overwhelming force of real existence, and also as a disembodied spirit among the shades:

> "And that's the end. He passes away under a cloud, inscrutable at heart, forgotten, unforgiven, and excessively romantic. Not in the wildest days of his boyish visions could he have seen the alluring shape of such an extraordinary success! For it may very well be that in the short moment of his last proud and unflinching glance, he had beheld the face of that opportunity which, like an Eastern bride, had come veiled to his side.
>
> "But we can see him, an obscure conqueror of fame, tearing himself out of the arms of a jealous love at the sign, at the call of his exalted egoism. He goes away from a living woman to celebrate his pitiless wedding with a shadowy ideal of conduct. Is he satisfied—quite, now, I wonder? We ought to know. He is one of us—and have I not stood up once, like an evoked ghost, to answer for his

eternal constancy? Was I so very wrong after all? Now he is no more, there are days when the reality of his existence comes to me with an immense, with an overwhelming force; and yet upon my honour there are moments, too, when he passes from my eyes like a disembodied spirit astray amongst the passions of his earth, ready to surrender himself faithfully to the claim of his own world of shades.

"Who knows? He is gone, inscrutable at heart, and the poor girl is leading a sort of soundless, inert life in Stein's house. Stein has aged greatly of late. He feels it himself, and says often that he is 'preparing to leave all this; preparing to leave . . .' while he waves his hand sadly at his butterflies."

Stein's sadness is that he had hoped to find a successor in Jim and now wanes into the sense that he is at the end of a tradition. Enigmatic as always, Marlow cannot resolve his own attitude towards Jim. I do not suppose that we can either and I wonder if that is necessarily an aesthetic strength in Conrad's novel. Perhaps it is enough that we are left pondering our own inability to reconcile the authentic and the heroic.

The Truth in the Well

Elliott B. Gose, Jr.

Of the four novelists closely considered in [*Imagination Indulged*],
Conrad was the most self-consciously artistic. Partly this was historical: he lived during a time when the novel was beginning to be
taken seriously as a literary form. But more to the point, as we saw
in the last chapter, Conrad was temperamentally self-conscious,
obliged to scrutinize motives and methods. The first sentence of the
preface to *The Nigger of the "Narcissus"* could be said to stand as a
paradigm not only of his aesthetics but of his psychology and philosophy: "A work that aspires . . . to the condition of art should
carry its justification in every line." Conrad himself, we may gloss,
carried the burden of justifying his life from the time of his escapades
in Marseilles. Thematically and artistically, his work was the highest
expression of this need to justify. *Lord Jim* seems to me of all these
attempts the most ambitious—"the most satanically ambitious" as
Conrad confided to a friend. Any work of art is satanic insofar as it
attempts to create another universe, especially one operating on laws
different from God's. Conrad as a lapsed Catholic would have been
well aware of this view. In fact, I would like to suggest that he tried
to embody the dilemma in his novel. In the first half of *Lord Jim,* he
presented us with an egoist trying to cope with the social world. In
the second half, he allowed the egoist to withdraw into himself,
satanically to set up his own kingdom. Then he asked, Can such a
world of romance stand up on its own terms, transcending the con-

From *Imagination Indulged: The Irrational in the Nineteenth-Century Novel.* © 1972 by
McGill-Queen's University Press.

ventional world? Conrad had doubts that he had successfully asked
the question or presented the problem. We may therefore expect to
have to exert ourselves if we want to understand what is going on in
Lord Jim.

Our first task is to try to understand the opposed conceptions of
the first and second halves of the novel. The *Patna* episode demon-
strates that the beliefs men share govern their fate, while the Patusan
sequence tests the possibility that one man's imagination can determine his fate. The Western world of the *Patna* is dominated by
Marlow's moral principles; the Eastern world of Patusan appears to
function according to Jim's application of Stein's romantic prescription. Marlow delivers his code in chapter 5, immediately after his
introduction. Jim, he says, as "one of us" should have "that inborn
ability to look temptations straight in the face—a readiness unintel-
lectual enough, goodness knows, but without pose—a power of
resistance . . . —an unthinking and blessed stiffness before the outward and inward terrors . . . backed by a . . . belief in a few simple
notions."

For Marlow, as we saw in the last chapter, the central notion is
fidelity to "the craft of the sea . . . the craft whose whole secret could
be expressed in one short sentence, and yet must be driven afresh
every day into young heads till it becomes the component part of
every waking thought—till it is present in every dream of their young
sleep!" The implications of this statement are far reaching. A good
sailor must be alert and conscious of detail. In fact he must reshape
his unconscious life to the image of his consciousness of the outside.
Formulated in this way, Marlow's belief stands directly opposed to
Stein's basic principle that "a man that is born falls into a dream like
a man who falls into the sea." Stein, an initiate into the secret lore of
adventure, advises living from the dream. Marlow, speaking for
responsibility but also for Western materialism, emphasizes the need
to understand and master outside reality. Of the situation that pre-
cipitated Jim's jump from the *Patna,* Marlow says, "It was all threats,
all a terribly effective feint, a sham from beginning to end, planned
by the tremendous disdain of the Dark Powers whose real terrors,
always on the verge of triumph, are perpetually foiled by the steadfastness of men."

Human solidarity is only one part of Marlow's code; the bond
with the visible universe is equally important. Simply, a sailor must
be responsive to the elements and to his ship. Jim is unable to give his

full attention to them. "He had to bear the criticism of men, the exactions of the sea, and the prosaic severity of the daily task that gives bread—but whose only reward is in the perfect love of the work. This reward eluded him." Instead of showing a concern for the demanding but necessary routine of the ship or for his duty to the passengers, Jim spends his time in daydreams of heroism. These dreams are intensified when he arrives in the East. He is lulled by "the softness of the sky, the languor of the earth, the bewitching breath of the Eastern waters. There were perfumes in it, suggestions of infinite repose, the gift of endless dreams."

Appropriately enough, those who live in the East have evolved a religion which includes this gift of the region. The eight hundred Moslem pilgrims stream on to the *Patna* "urged by faith and the hope of paradise." They journey "at the call of an idea . . . the unconscious pilgrims of an exacting belief." These pilgrims have made the dream their reality. They are as true to it as Marlow is to the demands of his reality and are therefore as successful in achieving their goal. The opposition between Western and Eastern man can be seen initially, then, as the opposition already mentioned between conscious and unconscious. In fact the pilgrims' way of life embodies one version of Stein's philosophy; they have so far submitted to the unconscious as to be identified with the sea. They "spread on all sides over the deck, flowed forward and aft, overflowed down the yawning hatchways, filled the inner recesses of the ship—like water filling a cistern, like water flowing into crevices and crannies, like water rising silently even with the rim." Western man, on the other hand, rises above the sea, as seen in one of several contrasts Conrad makes between the Western and Eastern ways of life. "The Arab standing up aft, recited aloud the prayer of travellers by sea. He invoked the favour of the Most High upon that journey, implored His blessing on men's toil and on the secret purposes of their hearts; the steamer pounded in the dusk the calm water of the Strait; and far astern of the pilgrim ship a screw-pile lighthouse, planted by unbelievers on a treacherous shoal, seemed to wink at her its eye of flame, as if in derision of her errand of faith."

The lighthouse is the epitome of Western man, symbolizing as it does his attempt to penetrate the darkness, to enable himself to steer a safe course through the dangerous unknown, to safeguard the future by rearranging the materials of nature and giving them conscious shape through the light of reason. It winks in derision at the faith of the pilgrims because, where they give themselves up to an inscrutable God (the word *Islam* means "submission"), Western man sets out to subdue the unknown, to impose the light of conscious reason on all dark and treacherous realms.

Balancing the demands of the inner and outer worlds was a preoccupation with Conrad. In 1903, for instance, he wrote to a Polish friend of his artistic aim, "It is difficult to depict faithfully in a work of imagination that innermost world as one apprehends it, and to express one's own real sense of that inner life (which is the soul of human activity)." Conrad believed in human activity, but as something done physically. In his writing he was always concerned to give expression to those patterns of the inner self which are the shaping spirit of such activity.

Jim, from this point of view, has the wrong type of soul to grapple effectively with the problems raised by the crisis on the *Patna*. Conrad therefore presents him with Patusan, a world ordered according to Stein's romantic philosophy. Even Marlow says of Patusan that there "the haggard utilitarian lies of our civilisation wither and die, to be replaced by pure exercises of imagination, that have the futility, often the charm, and sometimes the deep hidden truthfulness, of works of art." As I see Conrad's aim in the second half of *Lord Jim*, it was to present a picture of the land of the imagination, to give a true rendering of the large and autonomous forces that reign there.

In fact, I believe that Conrad constructed Patusan on principles strikingly similar to those later used by Jung to analyse the structure of what he called the collective unconscious. Briefly, Jung believed that where psychic energy can not "flow into life at the right time [it] regresses to the mythical world of the archetypes, where it activates images which, since the remotest times, have expressed the non-human life of the gods, whether of the upper world or the lower." Jung saw these images as unconscious personas, "certain types which deserve the name of dominants. These are archetypes like the anima, animus, wise old man, witch, shadow, earth-mother, . . . and the organizing dominants, the self, the circle, and the quarternity, i.e., the four functions or aspects of the self or of consciousness" (*Symbols of Transformation*). As an empiricist, Jung admitted that these figures are a metaphorical way of talking about mental processes, but he also insisted that whether by definition or by observation unconscious processes cannot be known except through metaphor (as they are expressed, for instance, in dreams). In any case, we can see these traditional personified forms as part of a pattern which throws considerable light on Jim's experience in Patusan.

First we should note the presence of a Jungian figure that we have already met, the wise old man. Although *Lord Jim* has a number of helpful, fatherly figures, only one, Stein, fits the following description by Jung:

> Often the old man in fairy tales asks questions like who? why? whence? and wither? for the purpose of inducing self-reflection and mobilizing the moral forces, and more often still he gives the necessary magical talisman, the unexpected and improbable power to succeed, which is one of the peculiarities of the unified personality in good or bad alike. But the intervention of the old man—the spontaneous objectivation of the archetype—would seem to be equally indispensable, since the conscious will by itself is hardly ever capable of uniting the personality to the point where it acquires this extraordinary power to succeed.

Stein sees immediately that Jim is romantic, thinks of Patusan as the place to send him, and gives him the ring which is "the necessary magical talisman" that opens up Patusan for Jim's improbable success. In contrast, Marlow, representing the strength of the conscious mind, comes to realize that, for all his fatherly good intentions, the opportunities he has given Jim were "merely opportunities to earn his bread."

In a letter to Edward Garnett, Conrad voiced agreement with his friend's criticism of *Lord Jim:* "I've been satanically ambitious, but there's nothing of a devil in me, worse luck." In fact, however, Conrad was well aware that he had at least a daimon inside him, an *alter ego* which had long known adventures in the interior world. Patusan seems to me the equivalent of that world, and Stein the magician who makes it come alive for Jim. In the same letter to Garnett, Conrad admitted that he had "wanted to obtain a sort of lurid light out (of) the very events" in *Lord Jim*. The word "lurid" is exactly the right word to characterize the tone of the second half of the novel. Conrad's conception of Patusan was, as I see it, intentionally romantic and archetypal. The nature of the action there is thus clearly to be contrasted with, but not necessarily judged by, the more realistic action of the first part of the novel.

As a preliminary to an archetypal analysis of Patusan, let us consider Stein's romantic prescription. "A man that is born falls into a dream like a man who falls into the sea. If he tries to climb out into the air as inexperienced people endeavour to do, he drowns." So "the way is to the destructive element submit yourself, and with the exertions of your hands and feet in the water make the deep, deep sea keep you up." As noted already, this approach is the opposite of Marlow's realistic desire to drive "the craft of the sea" into the minds of young seamen "till it is present in every dream of their young sleep." Marlow would make the inner world over to the demands of the outer; Stein would keep asserting the inner until it works in the outer, "to follow the dream, and again to follow the dream."

Stein's own past offers a good illustration of this process. A hunter of butterflies, he had long looked for a specimen of a certain rare species. "I took long journeys and underwent great privations; I . . . dreamed of him in my sleep," but he never found one until he gave himself over to the life of a native state in which he went as a Western trader. He became a close friend of the ruler, took his sister as wife, and had a daughter by her. Then riding alone he was ambushed by his friend's enemies. Still acting as a man engaged in that life (rather than in the Western one of laws), Stein immersed himself in the destructive element by feigning death, waiting until his attackers drew near, then killing three of them. As he looked at the third "for some sign of life I observed something like a faint shadow pass over his forehead. It was the shadow of this butterfly." It is the rare one, and he catches it.

The parallel with Jim's experience in Patusan is evident. He also gives himself to the life of the native state to which Stein sends him. He conceives a plan to help Stein's old "war-comrade," Doramin, by defeating the destructive force of Sherif Ali. Just after convincing Doramin's followers to follow his plan, he has to face a plot on his life. "Jim's slumbers were disturbed by a dream of heavens like brass resounding with a great voice, which called upon him to Awake! Awake! so loud that, notwithstanding his desperate determination to sleep on, he did wake up in reality." He is warned of the coming attempt on his life by the stepdaughter of Cornelius, the treacherous man with whom he is staying. When he refuses her advice to flee to Doramin, she leads him to the storeroom in which he thinks the assassins may be hiding. At first the room appears empty; then from under the mats emerges a man with a sword; "his naked body glistened as if wet." Confidently, Jim withholds his fire so long that when he shoots the man falls dead "just short of Jim's bare toes." Immediately, Jim finds "himself calm, appeased, without rancour, without uneasiness, as if the death of that man had atoned for everything." Then another assassin crawls out of the mats. "You want your life?" Jim said. The other made no sound. 'How many more of you?' asked Jim again. 'Two more, Tuan,' said the man very softly, looking with big fascinated eyes into the muzzle of the revolver. Accordingly two more crawled from under the mats, holding out ostentatiously their empty hands." He takes the three to the river, where (unconsciously) he makes them enact his own earlier desertion of duty. " 'Jump!' he thundered. The three splashes made one splash, a shower flew up, black heads bobbed convulsively, and disappeared; . . . Jim turned to the girl, who had been a silent and attentive observer. His heart seemed suddenly to grow too big for his breast . . . and the calm soft starlight descended upon them, unchecked." Just as Stein has found his treasure after immersing in the destructive element and following his dream where it led him, so Jim under parallel circumstances finds his in the girl to whom he gives a name "that means precious, in the sense of a precious gem—jewel." And Jewel she is called.

This name is responsible for a mistake which illustrates Marlow's comment that the native mind replaces "the haggard utilitarian lies of our civilisation" with "pure exercises of imagination that have . . . sometimes the deep hidden truthfulness of works of art." During a conversation with a man on the coast south of Patusan, Marlow hears about "a mysterious white man in Patusan who had got hold of an extraordinary gem—namely, an emerald of an enormous size, and altogether priceless." More, "such a jewel—it was explained to me by the old fellow from whom I heard most of this amazing Jim-myth . . . is best preserved by being concealed about the person of a woman." If there were such a woman, always close to Jim, "there could be no doubt she wore the white man's jewel concealed upon her bosom." Looking at the "Jim-myth" from a Jungian point of view, Jewel is clearly the anima.

The anima is Jung's term for a conception "for which the expression 'soul' is too general and too vague" ("Aion," *Psyche and Symbol*). For a man it stands as the feminine counterpart of his consciously masculine nature. "The anima personifies the total unconscious so long as she is not differentiated as a figure from the other archetypes. With further differentiations the figure of the (wise) old man becomes detached from the anima and appears as an archetype of the 'spirit' " (*Symbols of Transformation*). The situation which causes these manifestations to appear is lack of inner harmony. Once faced the problem may be resolved. "If this situation is dramatized, as the unconscious usually dramatizes it, then there appears before you on the psychological stage a man living regressively, seeking his childhood and his mother, fleeing from a cold cruel world which denies him understanding" ("Aion"). Since the last part of this statement obviously suits Jim, let us see if the first part about regression toward the mother does.

Conrad certainly goes out of his way to indicate a quality of childishness in Jim in Patusan. Chapter 34 ends with Cornelius's biased comment on him, "No more than a little child—a little child." But chapter 35 ends with a similar comment by Marlow; as he sails away, Jim appears "no bigger than a child." And earlier, Marlow's description of Jim with Jewel strikes the same odd note. " 'Hallo, girl!' he cried, cheerily. 'Hallo, boy!' she answered at once. . . . This was their usual greeting to each other." A clue to the reason for such behaviour is also given by Jung; it is that a person regresses, or goes back toward childhood, in order to start again. But before he can start again he must be reborn.

We may see Jim's second chance really beginning just after he makes his two jumps into the real life of Patusan: In the first he goes "like a bird" over the stockade in which he has been a prisoner of the Rajah, and in the second he jumps across the creek which separates him from Doramin, landing "in an extremely soft and sticky mudbank."

> The higher firm ground was about six feet in front of him. "I thought I would have to die there all the same," he said. He reached and grabbed desperately with his hands, and only succeeded in gathering a horrible cold shiny heap of slime against his breast—up to his very chin. It seemed to him he was burying himself alive, and then he struck out madly, scattering the mud with his fists. It fell on his head, on his face, over his eyes, into his mouth. . . . He arose muddy from head to foot and stood there, thinking he was alone of his kind for hundreds of miles, alone, with no help, no sympathy, no pity to expect from any one.

He is wrong, however; as soon as he produces the ring, he is accepted by Doramin and his followers, who give him the sympathy and aid that a helpless child needs. "He was safe. Doramin's people were barricading the gate and pouring water down his throat; Doramin's old wife, full of business and commiseration, was issuing shrill orders to her girls. 'The old woman,' he said, softly, 'made a to-do over me as if I had been her own son. They put me into an immense bed—her state bed—and she ran in and out wiping her eyes to give me pats on the back." As Jung puts it, "He who stems from two mothers is the hero: the first birth makes him a mortal man, the second an immortal half-god" (*Symbols of Transformation*). On the simplest archetypal level, then, Jim's heroic success-to-come with the assassins, with Jewel, with Sherif Ali's force can all be accounted for by his having found the right way to begin his second chance.

Jim's jump into the mud bears some resemblance to the mythical hero's plunge into darkness as well as to the rejuvenation process of many fairy tales. We have already seen [elsewhere] the youth in "Iron Hans" dip his hair in the well of purity. In the similar Norwegian tale of "The Widow's Son," as in the Russian "Fire-Bird," the hero plunges into a boiling cauldron and emerges young, fresh, and strong. That Conrad knew of such tales is evident from a letter he wrote Hugh Walpole during World War I. "I have been (like a sort of dismal male witch) peering (mentally), into the cauldron into which *la force des choses* has plunged you bodily. What will come of it? A very subtle poison or some very rough-tested Elixir of Life? Or neither?" (*Life and Letters*). We can find in fairy tales all three of these motifs of magical peering, plunging, and drinking. The latter along with the key word, "elixir," makes an appearance in *Lord Jim*, in an ironic metaphoric description by Marlow of Jim's reaction to the "legend of strength and prowess, forming round his name" in Patusan. "Felicity, felicity—how shall I say it?—is quaffed out of a golden cup. . . . He was of the sort that would drink deep, . . . flushed with the elixir at his lips." But the second motif of "plunging into" is the one that applies best to Jim's jump. If Conrad had plunged Jim in water instead of mud, he would not only have come closer to the conventional model of heroic transformation, he would also have made the incident fit better Stein's prescription, "in the destructive element immerse." Why did he choose this other way?

The most obvious explanation is an experience of Conrad's own.

According to his wife, when he was in the Congo, in 1890, he was involved in a terrifying accident. Running a steamboat on the river,

> he had sent his boys ashore to cut wood. . . . After a time he heard shots and sounds of quarrelling. Seizing his rifle— and his whistle, which he hung round his neck, he started to look for them. Almost before he had gone ten yards from the bank his feet sank into a deep bog, he fired all his cartridges without attracting any attention from the two men left on board the steamer, and sank steadily deeper and deeper. He was already as deep as his armpits, when he bethought himself of the whistle. At the third shrill note he saw two men running towards him with boughs and he swooned. His next recollection was finding himself strapped to a chair on the bridge and the steamer already underway.

Conrad told the anecdote after Mrs. Conrad found the whistle, still on its string. We might remember that it is on a string round his neck that Jim puts the ring which will save his life in Patusan. Conrad's accident can help to explain the overtones of burial and death noticeable when rebirth is suggested not only in *Lord Jim,* but also in *The Nigger of the "Narcissus"* and in *Heart of Darkness.*

But there is more to this thematic cluster than can be seen in one accident in Conrad's life. The other possibilities come out interestingly in the letter to Edward Garnett on *Lord Jim.* "I admit I stood for a great triumph and I have only succeeded in giving myself utterly away. Nobody'll see it, but you have detected me falling back into my lump of clay I had been lugging up from the bottom of the pit, with the idea of breathing big life into it. . . . The *Outcast* is a heap of sand, the *Nigger* a splash of water, *Jim* a lump of clay. A stone, I suppose will be my next gift to the impatient mankind—before I get drowned in mud to which even my supreme struggles won't give a simulacrum of life" (*Letters to Garnett*). The phrase, "drowned in mud," provides an obvious connection with the accident described by Mrs. Conrad, while the images of birth restore the connection between such an immersion and life. What in Jim's experience is connected with rebirth is in Conrad's connected with creation. Nor is the psychoanalytic correlation far to seek. As the phrases "heap of sand," "lump of clay," and "a stone" indicate, Conrad's gifts to mankind are of an anal nature. Rather than a cause for outrage, however, we may take that nature as a compliment to his readers. Although one obvious use of anal imagery is aggressive and destructive, another use is also recognized in psychiatry. This second use is creative, perhaps in males a substitute for the female's ability to give birth. As Jung comments, in myths, "the first men were made from earth or clay. The Latin *lutum,* which really means 'mud,' also had the metaphorical meaning of 'filth' " (*Symbols of Transformation*).

If we now look again at Jim's action in the mudbank we can appreciate an important passage not quoted before. Jim made efforts "culminating into one mighty supreme effort in the darkness to crack the earth asunder, to throw it off his limbs—and he felt himself creeping feebly up the bank. He lay full length on the firm ground and saw the light, the sky." Although he then goes on to Doramin's wife still "beplastered with filth out of all semblance to a human being," he has already been born, has thrown off the earth and moved from darkness to light on his own. As Jung notes, in this process of self-transformation into the hero, the individual becomes more intimately connected with the mother, but becomes independent of and equal to the father. In Jungian terms, the hero assimilates the archetype of the wise old man in the process of becoming "his own father and his own begetter" (*Symbols of Transformation*). Where, before, Jim had been grateful for and followed the advice of such father figures as Marlow and Stein, after his rebirth he himself becomes the advice-giver, the planner, the law-giver. He overshadows all fathers: Cornelius ("in-law"), the Rajah (political), Sherif Ali (religious), and even Doramin, whose son becomes Jim's brother.

As we know, however, it is Doramin who shoots Jim at the end of the novel. How are we to treat as a hero someone whose life ends as Jim's does? One answer lies within the archetypal framework through which we have approached his experience. In our analysis so far we have omitted one important figure, the shadow, which in Jung's system stands for all the unfavourable characteristics of an individual which are repressed from conscious knowledge. Rather than disappearing, these unacknowledged dark traits tend to take on a life of their own. "The shadow is a moral problem that challenges the whole ego personality, for no one can become conscious of the shadow without considerable moral effort. To become conscious of it involves recognizing the dark aspects of the personality as present and real" ("Aion"). It is here that Jim's weakness lies. He cannot admit his kinship with the disreputable characters whom he accompanies in deserting the *Patna*. He stands trial in the hope of distinguishing himself from them, but his failure in analysis is precisely moral, in Marlow's opinion. Although Marlow grants that Jim is trying to "save from the fire his idea of what his moral identity should be," he comes to believe that Jim "had no leisure to regret what he had lost, he was so wholly and naturally concerned for what he had failed to obtain." Marlow tries unsuccessfully to make Jim aware of his moral failure. Stein, however, without concerning himself with that side of the problem, simply sends Jim into a situation in Patusan where he can obtain his desired heroism. Jim's success is therefore achieved without his ever coming to terms with his shadow.

According to Jungian theory, this move simply strengthens the shadow. Unrecognized within, it appears without as an alter ego which will isolate the individual from his environment. The person who takes on this role in Jim's life is Gentleman Brown. He is obviously a villain, but as Jim's shadow he is able to hit with uncanny accuracy on the words which immobilize Jim and keep him from dealing effectively with that villainy. As Marlow characterizes Brown's verbal approach to Jim, it contains "a vein of subtle reference to their common blood, an assumption of common experience; a sickening suggestion of common guilt, of secret knowledge that was like a bond of their minds and of their hearts." This dark, private bond, which is the inverse of public solidarity, culminates in Brown's act of treachery—which, in Marlow's evaluation, has its inverse morality. "It was a lesson, a retribution—a demonstration of some obscure and awful attribute of our nature which, I am afraid, is not so very far under the surface as we like to think."

In killing Dain Waris, the son of Doramin, Brown disrupts the harmony that Jim created and maintained in his archetypal land. Jim has two choices. He can flee with Jewel and a few followers, or he can maintain the pledge he made to Doramin, to "answer with his life for any harm" that Brown and his men might do if allowed to go free. In keeping his word, Jim has to give up the authority he has exercised in Patusan. He gives it back to Doramin, from whom he had taken it. But what he activates in doing so is a side of Doramin's nature which had lain dormant as long as Jim was in command.

In Marlow's first description of Doramin, we hear that he has a "throat like a bull." When his son's body is brought to him, Doramin is silent until shown Jim's silver ring, which was on the forefinger of Dain Waris because Jim had sent it to him as "a token" of the importance of giving Brown a clear passage down the river. At sight of the ring, Doramin gives "one great fierce cry, deep from the chest, a roar of pain and fury, as mighty as the bellow of a wounded bull." Then when Jim confronts him, "the unwieldy old man, lowering his big forehead like an ox under a yoke, made an effort to rise, clutching at the flintlock pistols on his knees. From his throat came gurgling, choking, inhuman sounds, and his two attendants helped him from behind. People remarked that the ring which he had dropped on his lap fell and rolled against the foot of the white man, and that poor Jim glanced down at the talisman that had opened for him the door of fame, love, and success." In one sense, then, Jim dies a sacrifice to the subhuman side of human nature as represented in Doramin's destructive animality, and in that of Brown, whom Marlow had described as "bowed and hairy . . . like some man-beast of folklore." Since Brown is Jim's alter ego, we realize that Jim, the idealist who dresses in pure white, is the victim of his own repressed brute nature.

But, from Jim's point of view, he sacrifices himself to gain the higher goal he has desired. As Marlow puts it, after Brown's act Jim determines that "the dark powers should not rob him twice of his peace." Jim had known such a state on the *Patna,* the "high peace of sea and sky" which allowed his thoughts to "be full of valorous deeds." In such an atmosphere, "the eternity beyond the sky seemed to come down nearer to the earth, with the augmented glitter of the stars." Conrad had himself experienced this same feeling when he first went to sea: "In my early days, starting out on a voyage was like being launched into Eternity. . . . An enormous silence, in which there was nothing to connect one with the Universe but the incessant wheeling about of the sun and other celestial bodies, the alternation of light and shadow, eternally chasing each other over the sky. The time of the earth, though most carefully recorded by the half-hourly bells, did not count in reality." Earth and its time were exactly what Jim left behind when he dropped the clock he was mending and jumped out of the Rajah's stockade. Here is Conrad's description of the second jump: "The earth seemed fairly to fly backwards under his feet." And here is Marlow's preview of Jim achieving success in Patusan: "Had Stein arranged to send him into a star of the fifth magnitude the change could not have been greater. He left his earthly failings behind him and . . . there was a totally new set of conditions for his imaginative faculty to work upon."

But, when those earthly, animal failings intrude even into this world, Jim chooses to "prove his power in another way and conquer the fatal destiny itself." He must move on to yet another world and find his anima or soul in an eternal realm where no shadows exist. Marlow speculates, "it may very well be that in the short moment of his last proud and unflinching glance, he had beheld the face of that opportunity which, like an Eastern bride, had come veiled to his side."

Like Eustacia Vye, Jim may be seen as having found through death "an artistically happy background." But Conrad, like Hardy, felt quite ambiguous about his self-centered hero. Whereas Hardy expressed his reservations in direct comments, Conrad demonstrated his by creating a narrator with an outlook diametrically opposed to Jim's. Needless to say, Marlow's temperament has its effect in the characterization not just of Jim but of Stein and Jewel, and of Patusan. Marlow puts his position most graphically in the form of an opposition between images. In Patusan he watches the moon rise

> like an ascending spirit out of a grave; its sheen descended, cold and pale, like the ghost of dead sunlight. There is something haunting in the light of the moon; it has all the dispassionateness of a disembodied soul, and something of its inconceivable mystery. It is to our sunshine, which— say what you like—is all we have to live by, what the echo is to the sound: misleading and confusing whether the note be mocking or sad. It robs all forms of matter—which, after all, is our domain—of their substance, and gives a sinister reality to shadows alone.

The images present here—"grave" and "ghost," "spirit" and "shadow"—Marlow uses many times to characterize Jim, Jewel, and Stein. The aim of this use is to undercut the validity of Jim's life in Patusan, and of the romanticism which made Jim's heroism possible.

The process of undercutting begins in Marlow's original conversation with Stein. Just before Stein delivers his romantic prescription, Marlow describes him: "His tall form, as though robbed of its substance, hovered noiselessly over invisible things with stooping and indefinite movements; his voice, heard in that remoteness where he could be glimpsed mysteriously busy with immaterial cares, was no longer incisive, seemed to roll voluminous and grave." It is from this recess, "out of the bright circle of the lamp into the ring of fainter light," that Stein discusses the value of the dream. The bright light is equivalent to the sun, the fainter light to the moon of Marlow's allegorical description of Patusan. The opposition between "concrete" and "immaterial" is again emphasized.

It is in such a context that Stein propounds his solution for Jim's problem. And, as he finishes it, Marlow gives us his reaction. "The light had destroyed the assurance which had inspired him in the distant shadows. . . . The whisper of his conviction seemed to open before me a vast and uncertain expanse, as of a crepuscular horizon on a plain at dawn—or was it, perchance, at the coming of the night? One had not the courage to decide; but it was a charming and deceptive light throwing the impalpable poesy of its dimness over pitfalls—over graves." For a third time we have dim light connected with graves. Then Jim is mentioned, and something similar occurs when Stein suggests Patusan as a place to send him. Thinking of Jewel's mother, he says, "and the woman is dead now." Marlow comments, "Of course I don't know that story; I can only guess that once before Patusan had been used as a grave for some sin, transgression, or misfortune. It is impossible to suspect Stein."

When Marlow visits Patusan, he puts quite a bit of emphasis on this grave, and the relation of Jewel and Jim to it. Although the two lovers keep it up well, her mother's grave seems to Marlow to have a sinister appearance in the light of the moon. "It threw its level rays afar as if from a cavern, and in this mournful eclipse-like light the stumps of felled trees uprose very dark, the heavy shadows fell at my feet on all sides, my own moving shadow, and across my path the shadow of the solitary grave perpetually garlanded with flowers. . . . The lumps of white coral shone round the dark mound like a chaplet of bleached skulls." In view of these associations, it is not surprising that Marlow views Patusan as an unhealthy place for Jim to be, or that his final attitude toward Jim's decision to sacrifice himself is a suspicious one. "We can see him, an obscure conqueror of fame, tearing himself out of the arms of a jealous love at the sign, at the call of his exalted egoism. He goes away from a living woman to celebrate his pitiless wedding with a shadowy ideal of conduct."

If we look back as far as the *Patna* with Marlow's key images in mind, but without forgetting the later "Jim-myth," we can begin to see another possibility of interpreting those images. The sun, which Marlow takes as an image of what man has to live by, is not only present in the *Patna* episode; it is personified. "Every morning the sun, as if keeping pace in his revolutions with the progress of the pilgrimage, emerged with a silent burst of light exactly at the same distance astern of the ship, caught up with her at noon, pouring the concentrated fire of his rays on the pious purposes of the men, glided past on his descent, and sank mysteriously into the sea evening after evening." This early part of the novel is narrated by an impersonal voice presumably closer to Conrad's own than is Marlow's. In line with Conrad's impersonal philosophy, this voice describes the ship as suffering under the sun "as if scorched by a flame flicked at her from a heaven without pity. The nights descended on her like a benediction." In the night, "the propeller turned without a check, as though its beat had been part of the scheme of a safe universe." Though the universe is not safe, Jim mistakenly identifies with the night world rather than the day, and is betrayed when the *Patna* strikes a mysterious submerged object in the dark.

After he jumps, Jim looks back up at the *Patna*. " 'She seemed higher than a wall; she loomed like a cliff over the boat. . . . I wished I could die,' he cried. 'There was no going back. It was as if I had jumped into a well—into an everlasting deep hole. . . .' " (ellipses Conrad's). The wall, the cliff, and the hole are all images that reappear in the novel. Marlow picks them up immediately. "He had indeed jumped into an everlasting deep hole. He had tumbled from a height he could never scale again. By that time the boat had gone driving forward past the bows. It was too dark just then for them to see each other, and, moreover, they were blinded and half drowned with rain. He told me it was like being swept by a flood through a cavern." If we remember that Marlow had described the moon in Patusan as throwing "its level rays afar as if from a cavern," we can realize that in his opinion Jim, unlike Don Quixote, never does get out of the hole; he is buried there. As Jim himself puts it, "after the ship's lights had gone, anything might have happened in that boat. . . . We were like men walled up quick in a roomy grave." The question then becomes whether he can climb out.

Or as Conrad seems to have conceived it: can a man, once he has been buried, reappear *and live?* James Wait is rescued from his tomb in the *Narcissus,* but he must die and be committed to the deep before the ship reaches land. Kurtz is taken on board Marlow's ship in *Heart of Darkness* more dead than alive. Marlow says, "You should have heard the disinterred body of Mr. Kurtz." Later, "I looked at him as you peer down at a man who is lying at the bottom of a precipice where the sun never shines." Then he really dies, and Marlow is aware that "the pilgrims buried something in a muddy hole." Though Marlow is more intimately involved in the adventures of *Heart of Darkness*, Kurtz is a less sympathetic egoist than Jim; we must therefore simply note that a similar problem is posed in *Lord Jim*.

Before the *Patna* inquiry, we have a picture of Jim passing "days on the verandah, buried in a long chair, and coming out of his place of sepulture only at meal-times or late at night, when he wandered on the quays all by himself, detached from his surroundings, irresolute and silent, like a ghost without a home to haunt." The word "sepulture" should make us aware of the ironic allusion to Christ which is implicit in the experience of Jim, as it was in the rescue of James Wait. At first glance, this reference does not help us solve the problem because, although Christ rose from burial, like Wait and Kurtz, also like them he did not remain on earth long or substantially afterward. Jim does live long, but not, according to Marlow, substantially.

The Christ reference does provide a helpful clue, however, if we wish to connect Conrad's use of the sun with the various father figures in Jim's life. In *The Nigger of the "Narcissus"* Conrad referred to "the immortal sea" which in "its grace" insists that man labour rather than rest in peace. In *Lord Jim* he substitutes the sun as an image of God, but again it is "a heaven without pity." Sea and sun work together, however, in an interesting scene while Jim and the crew of the *Patna* are isolated in the life boat. Marlow reports that even Jim's "few mumbled words were enough to make me see the lower limb of the sun clearing the line of the horizon, the tremble of a vast ripple running over all the visible expanse of the sea, as if the waters had shuddered, giving birth to the globe of light, . . . I could imagine under the pellucid emptiness of the sky these four men imprisoned in the solitude of the sea, the lonely sun, regardless of the speck of life, ascending the clear curve of the heaven as if to gaze ardently from a greater height at his own splendour reflected in the still ocean." Lack of pity is still evident; it is joined by another characteristic.

The sun gazing "ardently . . . at his own splendour reflected in the still ocean" is presumably acting as the author of nature may. But we have quite a different situation when Marlow very soon after pictures for us a youth like Jim, just starting his career and "looking with shining eyes upon that glitter of the vast surface which is only a reflection of his own glances full of fire." Unlike the author of nature, the youth sees not reality but, according to Marlow, an "illusion" which is very "wide of reality." Although we have to take most of what Marlow reports as good evidence, we do not have to accept his interpretation of it. Accepting his view of the sun, we may ask ourselves whether it has to be the only standard of value. Why can we not see the hero, if he is brave enough and self-sufficient enough, becoming autonomous, born again to a cosmic destiny?

Something like this at any rate is what seems to happen after the sun had risen on the *Patna* lifeboat. Jim describes it. " 'The sun crept all the way from east to west over my bare head, but that day I could not come to any harm, I suppose. The sun could not make me mad. . . .' His right arm put aside the idea of madness. . . . 'Neither could it kill me. . . .' Again his arm repulsed a shadow. . . . '*That* rested with me' " (ellipses and italics Conrad's). He sums up, "I didn't bother myself at all about the sun over my head. I was thinking as coolly as any man that ever sat thinking in the shade." Jim has outfaced the sun, denied its authority, its right to punish him with the death that he suspects is its penalty for his crime. The result, however, seems to be that he is able to think on his own, "as coolly as any man that ever sat . . . in the *shade*." In other words, accepting Jim's testimony, we may want to see him as giving off his own light—see him as author, say, of the new life of Patusan. But we should see him as shining in areas not previously illumined, darkness being a figurative necessity for his assertion of authority.

Perhaps, then, we should not try to see Jim getting out of the hole into which he has jumped. Perhaps we should make a virtue of necessity and take the other image Jim offers us, the well, as offering something positive. James Wait was also in such a place; we are told that his rescuers "longed to abandon him, to get out of that place deep as a well" (*The Nigger*). This in itself is only an indication, but from Conrad's other writing it is evident that for him, as for Dickens, the image of the well had a special meaning. Conrad wrote in *A Personal Record* that fiction "after all is but truth often dragged out of a well and clothed in the painted robe of imaged phrases." Some indication of the location of this well came out in an ironic passage of a letter to John Galsworthy. "I shall keep the lid down on the well of my emotions. It's a question whether I even could lift it off. The hot spring boils somewhere deep within" (*Life and Letters*). We have already seen Conrad's contention that it is the artist's duty to "squeeze out" of himself "every sensation, every thought, every image" so that he finishes the day "*emptied* of every sensation and every thought," with "nothing left in" him (*Life and Letters*). I would urge, therefore, that the saying "Truth lies at the bottom of a well" can be taken as a more or less conscious epigraph for Conrad's aim and method as a writer.

To find the truth at the bottom of Jim's well will require, however, a little further digging. A well is often important in fairy tales. In "The Frog Prince" a princess loses her golden ball down a well, and finds there her husband-to-be. In "Iron Hans" we saw a young lad set to guard a well which gilds everything that is dipped in it. Similarly in "The Goose Girl at the Well," its water is associated with her golden hair that shines like sunbeams when she washes at the well. Most common, however, is the use of the well as a means to descend to another world, as in "Toads and Diamonds" or the similar "Mother Holle." In the latter it is again associated with gold, the good girl being showered with gold as she finally leaves this lower world into which she has jumped in despair. All of these tales are in Grimm, as is another common fairy-tale type, the three princesses abducted underground. In "The Gnome" the youngest of three huntsmen is lowered down a well by his two brothers. After defeating three dragons, he has the three princesses raised back up the well, but is treacherously stranded below by his brothers. He finds a flute, and when he blows it some elves appear; they take him back to the upper world where he is finally able to marry the youngest princess.

In *Lord Jim* Patusan is obviously the land at the bottom of the well where Jim, like the huntsman, can become the hero who rescues and destroys. But we must notice a crucial difference. In the fairy tale, despite serious obstacles, both to the rescue of the three princesses and to his return, the huntsman is able to accomplish both. Jim, however, is able to accomplish only the rescue. In his failure to return from the other world he breaks the pattern of the traditional hero of myth, fairy tale, or epic.

Jim succumbs to the danger expressed by Jung. If "regression occurs in a young person, his own individual life is supplanted by the divine archetypal drama, which is all the more devastating for him because his conscious education provides him with no means of recognizing what is happening, and thus with no possibility of freeing himself from its fascination" (*Symbols of Transformation*). In

Marlow's view, this is exactly what happens to Jim. "All his conquests, the trust, the fame, the friendships, the love—all these things
that made him master had made him a captive, too. He looked with
an owner's eye" at these things, "but it was they that possessed him
and made him their own to the innermost thought, to the slightest
stir of blood, to his last breath." We have to admit the pertinence of
this insight. Not only does "his last breath" push us ahead to Jim's
death, but "stir of blood" suggests that we associate that death with
an image immediately prefiguring it. "The sky over Patusan was
blood-red, immense, streaming like an open vein." Jim's death is a
direct result of his giving over authority to one of the archetypal
figures in that land. This act can now be seen not only as suicidal (so
that in Patusan he is both self-born and self-destroyed) but also as a
sacrifice to the sun as the ultimate author of life. For it is the sun
which makes the sky "blood-red," the same "western sun" which
Marlow claims makes "the coast" of Patusan look "like the very
stronghold of the night."

But suppose, being satisfied that Jim fails because he is in some
way not strong enough, we are still not willing to take Marlow's
analysis at face value. Suppose we feel that a "satanically ambitious"
Conrad must have intended a stronger romanticism than Marlow
condemns. In that case we must switch our critical perceptions to a
closer study of Marlow's own character.

Marlow is aware that his motives for getting involved with Jim
were suspect. He hoped through a "miracle" to discover behind the
obvious fact of Jim's dereliction of duty some means of meeting "the
doubt" it seems to cast on Marlow's own code, "the sovereign power
enthroned in a fixed standard of conduct." As indicated by the words
"fixed" and "enthroned," Marlow means a standard established and
upheld by public authority. His condemnation of Jim for upholding
a personal and hence "shadowy ideal of conduct" is therefore un-
derstandable. Marlow must, of course, be given high marks for his
persistent attempt to be sympathetic while telling Jim's story. But
the fact is that he lacks the one quality necessary to a real understanding of Jim. Marlow confesses, "As to me, I have no imagination (I would be more certain about him to-day, if I had)."

Remembering Marlow's evocation of the sun over the *Patna*
lifeboat or the moon over Patusan, we may be inclined to doubt this
statement. In fact it brings up the inevitable question of how much
of himself an author puts into a narrator. My belief is that much of

Marlow's negative imagining (of which we are about to see more) expresses Conrad's own unconscious fears. But I also believe that Conrad consciously characterized Marlow as having an intellectual ability to construct favourable explanations of Jim's conduct which his emotions cannot accept.

In any case, right after denying his own imaginative faculty, Marlow goes on to give what seems to me quite clearly a warning to the reader. "He existed for me, and after all it is only through me that he exists for you. I've led him out by the hand; I have paraded him before you. Were my commonplace fears unjust? I won't say—not even now. You may be able to tell better, since the proverb has it that the onlookers see most of the game." One of the things that makes *Lord Jim* a great novel is the use to which Conrad put that insight, the number of characters whose views we are invited to absorb before coming to our own conclusions. That side of the novel concerns us, however, only as it applies to the principal narrator, Marlow. Conrad has him chivy his conventional listeners, as he did so successfully in *Heart of Darkness*. But in *Lord Jim* Marlow does not gain a deep emotional revelation, as he did in that shorter novel; rather Marlow specifically refuses a chance for involvement and possible enlightenment in the latter part of *Lord Jim*.

On the question of race, religion, and colour, the narrating voice of the early chapters is sympathetic to the dark Moslem pilgrims from the East. Marlow is much less so (as is the friend to whom he writes); he can speak only condescending praise of Jim's friendship for Dain Waris. But he does give us a clue when he mentions Dain Waris' "great reserves of intelligence and power. Such beings open to the Western eye, so often concerned with mere surfaces, the hidden possibilities of races and lands over which hangs the mystery of unrecorded ages." In *Heart of Darkness,* Marlow's active commitment to these "mere surfaces" saves him from "the reality" and "the inner truth, luckily, luckily." Marlow has no direct encounter with the barbaric tribes of the Congo; he learns vicariously through Kurtz. But in *Lord Jim,* the natives are not so barbaric, nor is it their truth which will corrupt Jim. In Patusan, therefore, Marlow's "mere surface" carries less dramatic and thematic weight than it did in the Congo. Marlow's clinging to it is consequently much less of a virtue in Patusan, as the comment on Dain Waris indicates.

The test of Marlow's clear-sightedness comes in his confronta-

tion with Jewel, which is to the second half of the novel what his
meeting with Jim is to the first. Ironically, in the first part of the
confrontation Marlow may be compared to Jim approaching his
destiny, the jump from the *Patna* into his hole. Looking into Jewel's
eyes, Marlow seems to see "a faint stir, such as you may fancy you
can detect when you plunge your gaze to the bottom of an im-
mensely deep well. What is it that moves there? you ask yourself. Is
it a blind monster or only a lost gleam from the universe? It occurred
to me—don't laugh—that all things being dissimilar, she was more
inscrutable in her childish ignorance that the Sphinx propounding
childish riddles to wayfarers." Like Jim, Marlow is offered a chance
to find truth at the bottom of a well. And, as in Marlow's relation to
Kurtz in *Heart of Darkness,* this chance comes in a vicarious form,
through another person. Jewel, like the Sphinx, asks a basic question
about her man. Less flattering to Marlow, she propounds an answer,
one that upsets him considerably. She suggests that Jim will prove
unfaithful to her. Marlow's reaction is to feel insecure. "The very
ground on which I stood seemed to melt under my feet."

Although all of Marlow's emphasis is on Jewel's irrational state,
the beginning of the scene makes it clear that Marlow has a problem,
too. All Jewel has to do is tell him the one reservation she had in
giving her love to Jim, and Marlow begins to feel threatened. "I
didn't want to die weeping," she says. " 'My mother had wept
bitterly before she died,' she explained. An inconceivable calmness
seemed to have risen from the ground around us, imperceptibly, like
the still rise of a flood in the night, obliterating the familiar land-
marks of emotions. There came upon me, as though I had felt myself
losing my footing in the midst of waters, a sudden dread, the dread
of the unknown depths." The description of the death that Jewel
then goes on to give is too much for Marlow.

> It had the power to drive me out of my conception of
> existence, out of that shelter each of us makes for himself
> to creep under in moments of danger, as a tortoise with-
> draws within its shell. For a moment I had a view of a
> world that seemed to wear a vast and dismal aspect of
> disorder, while, in truth, thanks to our unwearied efforts,
> it is as sunny an arrangement of small conveniences as the
> mind of man can conceive. But still—it was only a mo-
> ment: I went back into my shell directly. One *must*—don't

you know?—though I seemed to have lost all my words in the chaos of dark thoughts I had contemplated for a second or two beyond the pale. These came back, too, very soon, for words also belong to the sheltering conception of light and order which is our refuge.

At least three points here need comment.

First of all, we should notice that the sun has been reduced to a Polyanna adjective connected with "small conveniences." Marlow's irony in doing so is not really confident understatement, as his situation indicates. Second, we should notice that "words," like "light" and "order," have become a "refuge" rather than a means to truth.

And third, we should notice the image Marlow uses to describe his act of seeking refuge from the truth, "as a tortoise withdraws within its shell." This image appears only one other time in the novel, when Jim is in the lifeboat facing the sun. The other three deserters have "crept under" a boat-sail spread on the gunwales. After a while, the captain of the *Patna* "poked his big cropped head from under the canvas and screwed his fishy eyes up at me. 'Donnerwetter! you will die,' he growled, and drew in like a turtle." I don't believe the parallel is fortuitous, but even if it is, the larger parallel of the two incidents will hold. Faced with the threat of sinking in stormy waters or in a panicking sea of "unconscious pilgrims," the officers of the *Patna* take refuge in a lifeboat. Faced with the possibility of losing his mental "footing in the midst of dangerous waters" and "unknown depths," Marlow withdraws into "that shelter each of us makes for himself to creep under in moments of danger."

The only person to vary the pattern is Jim. He elects to sit outside the shelter, to face the trial, to go to the bottom of the well. He is not interested in "sunny" arrangements and "small conveniences." He is interested in words, light and order, but not as a "sheltering conception." Marlow himself finally puts Conrad's case directly: "The point, however, is that of all mankind Jim had no dealings but with himself, and the question is whether at the last he had not confessed to a faith mightier than the laws of order and progress." Jim's own faith obviously is "mightier" in the sense that he follows it with complete confidence at the end. Conrad expressed his own faith twelve years later in *A Personal Record*: "Only in men's imagination does every truth find an effective and undeniable existence. Imagination, not invention, is the supreme master of art as of life."

We may find it harder to accept Jim's desertion of Jewel. Marlow is willing before the end to face even that. "She had said he had been driven away from her by a dream,—and there was no answer one could make her—there seemed to be no forgiveness for such a transgression. And yet is not mankind itself, pushing on its blind way, driven by a dream of its greatness and its power upon the dark paths of excessive cruelty and of excessive devotion? And what is the pursuit of truth, after all?" The truth Jim is after does not lie in the "mere surfaces" usually scanned by "the Western eye." Rather it lies deep in his own sense of himself. If he discovers a flaw there which calls in doubt the harmony of that order, his decision to abide by the code he has established is at worst equivocal. A minor moral of the novel could certainly be that it is not for those who (like Marlow) are afraid to dip into the well of truth to condemn those who (like Jim) are drowned in the attempt to plumb its depths.

Perhaps Stein's original advice would have been clearer if it had begun "A romantic when he is born falls into a dream. . . ." From this point of view, we can understand why it is necessary for Jim to plunge in, and why it is not necessary for Marlow. We need also to remember that such a plunge was necessary for Conrad—as witness the late preface from which we have already quoted: "The romantic feeling of reality was in me an inborn faculty." Given a second chance after his misfortunes in Marseilles, Conrad, like Stein, settled down to the hard business of Western life. Then he gave himself a third chance, allowing the same imaginative faculty that had revelled in the adventures of his youth to create new and more lasting fictional adventures. Conrad's ambition was satanic in more than one way. As a writer who was at once romantic, realist, and impressionist, he aimed to create an ordered and almost tangible world of his own. And in his pride he wished to be honoured for his efforts.

The contrast between the man of action and the man of words was almost second nature to Conrad by the time he began his writing career. The man of action has to know the physical world, its necessities and its recalcitrance. He has to know how to work with other men, how to respect his bond with them. To this substantial world, and to the deserving people who populate it, Conrad naturally paid homage in description and in theme. But, in addition and behind this, in the very act of conception, he attempted "to depict faithfully" in each "work of imagination that innermost world . . . that inner life (which is the soul of human activity)."

In the light of such a confession, we should not be surprised if in one novel he not only chose a dreamer as his hero, but put him into a dream world to allow him to fight out there the very real conflicts which go on inside all of us. Nor is it improbable that, having chronicled Jim's failure, Conrad should yet have left open the likelihood that his hero had the right to make the choice he did.

An Intelligible Picture: *Lord Jim*

Peter J. Glassman

> *I've fitted the pieces together, and there is enough of them to make an intelligible picture.*
>
> —Marlow, *Lord Jim*

Conrad began *Lord Jim* during May or June of 1898, but interrupted work on the novel in December 1898 to write *Heart of Darkness*. He completed *Heart of Darkness* in February 1899 and returned to *Lord Jim* during the same month. The peculiar circumstance of their continuous composition, taken with their shared use of Marlow as both device and subject, narrator and character, suggests that *Heart of Darkness* and *Lord Jim* are connected acts of imagination, that the two novels are joined together in a common impulse and project.

That impulse, as I have remarked [elsewhere] about each of Conrad's earlier works, is autobiographical: the novel is chiefly interested in defining and sustaining the personality of its author. *Lord Jim,* though, separates itself from—and so concludes—the protracted process of self-elaboration which Conrad initiated ten years before by beginning *Almayer's Folly.* For if *Lord Jim* produces as its landscape an imagined universe fully as savage as that discovered in each of Conrad's earlier books, it as well develops a response to the earlier works' desperate situation, a mode of recovery from their crushing burden of disorder, loneliness, and pain. In this respect *Lord Jim* completes that era in Conrad's imagination of himself which I have tried to define in this study [*Language and Being*]. More important, the novel "justifies" at last the personality which, together with

From *Language and Being: Joseph Conrad and the Literature of Personality.* © 1976 by Peter J. Glassman.

Almayer's Folly, An Outcast of the Islands, The Nigger of the "Narcissus," and *Heart of Darkness,* it so "coherently" establishes.

I

Marlow and Stein agree that "man is amazing, but he is not a masterpiece." By this they mean to suggest that, unlike other creatures, man cannot satisfy the requirements of his imagination. As Stein puts the matter, " 'Sometimes it seems to me that man is come where he is not wanted, where there is no place for him.' " " 'We want in so many different ways to be,' " he explains:

> "[The] magnificent butterfly finds a little heap of dirt and sits still on it; but man will never on his heap of mud keep still. He want to be so, and again he want to be so. . . . He wants to be a saint, and he wants to be a devil—and every time he shuts his eyes he sees himself as a very fine fellow—so fine as he can never be."

One's "heart pain," Stein believes, is a function of one's power to achieve consciousness about oneself. " 'Because you not always can keep your eyes shut,' " he tells Marlow, " 'there comes the real trouble—the heart pain—the world pain. I tell you, my friend, it is not good for you to find you cannot make your dream come true, for the reason that you not strong enough are, or not clever enough. Ja!' "

It is a mistake, as Stein thinks, for one to resist the limitations of the human condition. He tells Marlow—it is, oddly, the novel's most celebrated occasion—that the sensible and successful man submits to the inevitability of dissatisfaction and commits his energy to the pedestrian imperative of simple survival:

> "A man that is born falls into a dream like a man who falls into the sea. If he tries to climb out into the air as inexperienced people endeavour to do, he drowns—*nicht wahr?* . . . No! I tell you! The way is to the destructive element submit yourself, and with the exertions of your hands and feet in the warm water make the deep, deep sea keep you up." (Conrad's ellipsis)

(In fact Stein feels considerably less able to accommodate "the world pain" than he suggests here. By the end of his evening discussion with Marlow, indeed, he confesses that he does not know how one ought to live: " 'So if you ask me—how to be?' . . . His twitching lips uttered no word, and the austere exultation of a certitude seen in the dusk vanished from his face.") Marlow consents to the injunction. What most is wanted in human life, he agrees, is not an unyielding assertion of individual appetite or need but an inexhaustible power of endurance—a power which he calls "the instinct of courage":

> I don't mean military courage, or civil courage, or any special kind of courage. I mean just that inborn ability to look temptations straight in the face—a readiness unintellectual enough, goodness knows, but without pose—a power of resistance, don't you see, ungracious if you like, but priceless—an unthinking and blessed stiffness before the outward and inward terrors, before the might of nature, and the seductive corruption of men.

This uncomplicated celebration of simple masculine probity invites mistrust. Modern readers are likely to react against an assumption which glorifies "stiffness" because it is an article of our shared persuasion that to suppress emotion is to inhibit the experience, and therefore the status, of the self. We normally maintain that those who could wish to circumscribe the range of human sensation secretly fear and despise life. But in their seemingly repressive moral attitudes Marlow and Stein do nothing but join themselves with the novel's mainstream of opinion. Captain Brierly, Captain Elliot, the French lieutenant—everyone of any established ethical authority in *Lord Jim* shares the two old friends' austere moral economy. And, indeed, there is nothing contemptible about the severe ethos with which *Lord Jim*'s fully situated people make communion. No one in the novel consciously wishes to restrict the experience of the self; they want rather to protect the self—and the community of selves—*from* experience. For the novel's people imagine other men and the outer world to be drastically dangerous. They respond in their endorsement of "unthinking and blessed stiffness" not to a brutal harshness of character, some fierce Murdstone delight in inhibition and repression, but to a universe which seems to each of them too perilous to support any less organized mode of being.

This impression of the universe is, of course, Conrad's own. It has shaped *Almayer's Folly, An Outcast of the Islands, The Nigger of the "Narcissus,"* and *Heart of Darkness,* and it forms the moral geography of *Lord Jim* as well. *Lord Jim,* indeed, makes programme of Conrad's terrified sense of other men's violence and iniquity. Time and again in its brief history the novel introduces episodes suggestive of the most gratuitous and terrible treachery, incidents of appalling and unpredictable reprobacy. The *Patna*'s swinish captain, the execrable Cornelius, Holy Terror Robinson, Sherif Ali, Rajah Tunku Allang, Gentleman Brown: *Lord Jim* is populated by a whole galaxy of chthonic creatures whose lives seem to represent a systematic crusade against human peace, solidarity, and dignity.

Nor is there anything, as one might say, "unnatural" about these people's dissoluteness. For in *Lord Jim,* as in each of Conrad's earlier novels, the universe itself seems organized in barely surreptitious, virtually animate opposition to human expectations and needs. As in each of his previous novels, Conrad in *Lord Jim* again imagines a geography of presented serenity which conceals enormously threatening and undivinable dangers; the novel's characters repeatedly are made to perceive their author's sense of "the suspended menace" at large "in the midst of the most perfect serenity." The sun, for instance, appears to experience actual malice against men. It looks splendid but its splendor is "sinister." It is said not merely to shine with extraordinary intensity and heat but "under a serene sky" to have "killed all thought, oppressed the heart, withered all impulses of strength and energy." Worse, the sun presumably is *pleased* to deplete men—as, evidently, it is pleased later in the book to "[dwarf] the earth into a mote of dust," or as the night is pleased to settle "silently on all the visible forms, effacing the outlines, burying the shapes deeper and deeper, like a steady fall of implacable black dust." Storms, too, operate in the novel as an instrument of the universe's vindictive malignancy. Evil deities of a sort, great winds strike the book's people as assaults deliberately directed against their irreducible impressions of peace, order, and personal primacy. Jim, for example, receives a gale at sea as an awesome attack upon his entire assumption of character:

> There was a fierce purpose in the gale, a furious earnestness in the screech of the wind, in the brutal tumult of earth and sky, that seemed directed at him, and made him hold his breath in awe.

The malice of the universe often is more subtle in the novel, though, and therefore more dangerous. Thus, it is in the clearest weather, during the most serene hour of a ship's day, that the *Patna,* as if by "a special arrangement of a malevolent providence," collides with a secreted hulk and in one instant shatters its crew's "great certitude of unbounded safety and peace." The ship's crew is destroyed in its sense of world and self with baleful suddenness, as if the universe were organized by a principle of "burlesque meanness," or directed by an intention to perform upon all men "a fiendish and appalling joke," "a joke hatched in hell," "an utterly aimless piece of devilry." (At one point in his narrative Marlow goes so far as to suggest that the universe in fact *is* controlled in its malignancy; that the world is organized by a conscious intelligence which wages open contest against humankind. "It was all threats," Marlow tells us, "all a terribly effective feint, a sham from beginning to end, planned by the tremendous disdain of the Dark Powers." Conrad refers to the "Dark Powers" with some frequency in his fiction. The phrase seems to me more a freedom of speech, though, than an assumption of philosophy, a grim reflex of humor directed against the difficulty of being human.) And the *Patna*'s experience is far from episodic in *Lord Jim*. All men, Marlow tells us, must be wary of the gentle forms of life. All men must suspect those evenings "of freshness and starlight that would make the best of us forget that we are only on sufferance here and got to pick our way in cross lights, watching every precious minute and every irremediable step."

If, then, men in *Lord Jim* are unpredictably and savagely mean to one another, if they often feel toward one another gratuitous and violent animosity, perhaps they take their cue from the malicious world in which they have their being—a world in which one is "tried more than is fair"; a world which feels against one "the jeering intention of a spiteful and vile vengeance," "a purpose of malice," an "unbridled cruelty . . . which means to smash, to destroy, to annihilate all [one] has seen, known, loved, enjoyed, or hated; all that is priceless and necessary." It is this universe which men must organize themselves to anticipate and to oppose in *Lord Jim*, and which Marlow's obdurate moral code addresses. It is exactly *because* "the unexpected always happens," as Marlow puts it, that he believes one steadfastly must maintain "an unthinking and blessed stiffness." It is because one cannot trust to the appearances of the world that, as Marlow believes, one must be able to trust one's own, and to "the sovereign power enthroned in a fixed standard of conduct." It is because "not one of us is safe" from "weaknesses that may lie hidden" in the universe and in the self that, as he thinks, one must organize and perhaps even circumscribe the self. Marlow, Brierly,

Elliot, the French lieutenant, even O'Brien, do not exalt sterility. They exalt, rather, what they take to be the protective power of a fixed moral assumption against the unfixed powers of the human personality and of the natural order which governs the personality. They want men, in a word, to be better than the world.

II

The great question in *Lord Jim*, then—in all of Conrad's fiction—is, in Marlow's phrase, "How to live," in Stein's, "How to be!" It is a problem which is brought into particular focus not by anything which Marlow or Stein themselves precisely do, but by the behavior—or, perhaps, by the very appearance—of Jim, the likely ship's mate who cravenly abandons a presumably sinking tub one stinking night on the Red Sea.

Because of his participation in his community's forced and rather desperate faith in mute "stiffness," Marlow initially is able to experience an uncomplicated reaction to Jim's conduct and an only slightly more complicated response to Jim himself. At first hearing, Jim's desertion of the *Patna* seems to Marlow unambiguous and unforgivable. Like Brierly, O'Brien, the French lieutenant, Marlow begins by believing absolutely in the preserving, if unwritten, sanction of his craft's code, which seems to him less a sweet gesture of civilized men than a sort of extramundane ordination. With his scandalized brethren Marlow shares an assured contempt toward Jim's effort to qualify the authority of that necessary and absolute canon. As Brierly puts it, " 'We must preserve professional decency or we become no better than so many tinkers going about loose.' "

Unlike his coevals, though, Marlow cannot sustain for long the purity of his censure. In fact, Marlow understands quite early in the novel that he feels troubled less by that which Jim has done than by the discrepancy between Jim's conduct and his wholesome appearance. For it has been an article of Marlow's faith that one may extend trust to certain attitudes of carriage, that manner and physiognomy are moral qualities. At least in their sordid mien Jim's sordid shipmates "somehow fitted the tale"; but Jim does not. He *looks* so forthright, reliable, and safe. In Marlow's famous phrase, "He was one of us":

I liked his appearance; I knew his appearance; he came from the right place; he was one of us. He stood there for all the parentage of his kind, for men and women by no means clever or amusing, but whose very existence is based upon honest faith, and upon the instinct of courage. . . . He was a youngster of the sort you like to see about you; of the sort you like to imagine yourself to have been; of the sort whose appearance claims the fellowship of those illusions you had thought gone out.

To Jim "on the strength of a single glance" Marlow "would have trusted the deck":

And, by Jove! it wouldn't have been safe. There are depths of horror in that thought. He looked as genuine as a new sovereign, but there was some infernal alloy in his metal. . . . I couldn't believe it. I tell you I wanted to see him squirm for the honour of the craft.

As it happens it is Marlow who most must squirm. For in his integrity he is quick to understand that Jim has exposed—exploded—the authority of his "craft." That craft, after all, supposes itself capable of recognizing infernal alloys. Failing that, it purports to neutralize such "alloys," to impart upon the weak an artificial capacity for steadfastness and resolve, to supply to the unfortunate an unearned "genuineness." Marlow understands that if his ethos so abjectly can fail so "promising a boy," that "if this sort can go wrong like that," Jim in some respects is correct to insist as peremptorily as he does that the universe admits of no firm supports—that no "fixed standard of conduct" can be proof against either the militant aggressiveness of the natural world or the shocking peccancy of the human mind.

"There are depths of horror in that thought" alone. What more unsettles Marlow, though, is his growing suspicion that his own "stiffness" perhaps is untrustworthy, his gradual perception that "if this sort can go wrong" so, certainly, can he. (It is in part to allay this fear that Marlow commits such an extravagant supply of energy and attention to Jim—as if by involving himself so intensely in Jim's situation he may discover circumstances which can justify the "boy's" behavior, and thus salvage the authority of "the craft." Marlow himself proposes this sense of his conduct: "Was it for my own sake that I wished to find some shadow of an excuse for that young fellow whom I had never seen before, but whose appearance alone added a touch of personal concern to the thoughts suggested by the knowledge of his weakness—made it a thing of mystery and terror—like a hint of a destructive fate ready for us all whose youth—in its day—had resembled his youth? I fear that such was the secret motive of my prying." Marlow has other, less conscious "motives," to which I shall return. Brierly, of course, cannot defend *himself* against the personal implications of Jim's failure.) Marlow never fully admits, as Jim wants him to do, that he should himself have abandoned the *Patna*. But this residual confidence cannot diminish his sense of personal "horror," for by argument and example Jim does convince him that conceivably he might do almost anything else. " 'Nobody, nobody is good enough,' " Marlow eventually confesses. One's "moral identity," he acknowledges at last, "[is] a convention, only one of the rules of the game, nothing more." (On several occasions Marlow seems to confess that about his own past he has much to justify—if not simply to suppress.)

III

If this be so, how is one to live? If not in accordance with a "fixed standard of conduct," how is one to be? As his previously untested investment in "the steadfastness of men" deteriorates, Marlow increasingly supposes that a human being more appropriately may be judged by the quality of his consciousness than by the propriety of his behavior. "Moral identity," he begins to assume, is knowable more by the complexity of one's sensibility than by the stolidity of one's comportment.

So it is that, as he is deprived by the events of the novel of his faith in "the instinct of courage," Marlow learns to direct his judgment against those characters in *Lord Jim* who seem to him deficient in feeling, observation, or perception. Thus, of all the novel's villains and degenerates he most unreservedly contemns those men "to whom the whole of life is like an after-diner hour with a cigar; easy, pleasant, empty." Jim's father, for example, suggests himself as an insignificant and foolish prater, full of "little thoughts about faith and virtue." In their systematic inauthenticity the novel's tourists seem to Marlow revolting, if vaguely comic. Cornelius strikes him as "a sinister pantaloon," "vermin-like." Chester and Robinson appear

"phantasmal and extravagant." The Rajah Allang seems "dirty, little, used-up, old . . . wizened grimy." The Sultan of Patusan "is an
imbecile youth with two thumbs on his left hand."

Marlow comes to believe, indeed, that such fatuousness as this
is nothing less than deliberate, that most men experience as the chief
impulse of their life the *desire* to avoid sensation. (Perhaps it is this
assumption which permits Marlow to suppose, extremely, that
"those who do not feel do not count.") He first indicts his direct
audience, but goes on to accuse us all of succumbing to an arid and
cowardly revulsion from affectual existence:

> The desire of peace waxes stronger as hope declines, till at
> last it conquers the very desire of life. Which of us here has
> not observed this, or maybe experienced something of that
> feeling in his own person—this extreme weariness of emo-
> tions, the vanity of effort, the yearning for rest?

It seems to Marlow that, seen from this point of view, particularly
"fixed standards of conduct" express the covert urge to neutralize
experience, the secret and manipulative wish to protect the self against
test or potentially painful investment of feeling. Thus, as he is ex-
panded in his own ethical consciousness by his increasing sympathy
for Jim's, Marlow feels himself estranged in an especially intense and
discomforting way from the novel's harbingers of fixed opinion.
The French lieutenant appears to him to be marked less by courage
or moral authority than by "stolid glibness." Brierly seems filled
with "self-satisfaction." The autonomically heroic Bob Stanton suggests himself as "a naughty youngster fighting with his mother." In
each of the communicants of his former faith Marlow principally
detects "the soft spot, the place of decay, the determination to lounge
safely through existence."

To the degree that he disestablishes the novel's other men
Marlow finds himself compelled to endow and to celebrate Jim. For
it seems to him that, if Jim has failed the first Marlovian "standard of
conduct," he from the first triumphantly survives the other. Jim,
after all, precisely refuses to be a "lounger": he always engages the
world, presses his arc, meets and contests that sad "desire of peace"
to which, as Marlow believes, everyone else accedes. Whatever else
he has done, Jim seems to Marlow "fine in the wildness of his
unexpressed, hardly formulated hope" that one may have one's will

and way with the brutally depersonalizing universe. "The thing is that," as Marlow puts it, "in virtue of his feeling [Jim] mattered":

> He had the gift of finding a special meaning in everything that happened to him. . . . I affirm that he had achieved greatness, . . . greatness as genuine as any man ever achieved.

Like Achilleus, Jim is able to say about his life, " 'I am satisfied . . . [Conrad's ellipsis] nearly. . . . I can stand it.' " In this respect he, at least, establishes himself in "imperishable reality"; he seems to Marlow the one being who has "come nearest to rising above the trammels of earthly caution":

> I had made up my mind that Jim, for whom alone I cared, had at last mastered his fate. He told me he was satisfied . . . nearly. [Conrad's ellipsis] This is going further than most of us dare. I—who have the right to think myself good enough—dare not. Neither does any of you here, I suppose?

(No doubt it is as an expression of this conviction that Marlow so often describes Jim as accumulating about himself all of the world's "sunshine" and "light.")

IV

The chief victim of Marlow's altered "ideal of conduct" obviously is Marlow himself. As his relationship with Jim progresses Marlow feels radically censorious toward himself, more at odds with his own "cautious" mode of being than with that of any other man. For he feels increasingly certain that, as measured against Jim's, his own experience is without quotient. Jim always has believed in the absolute authority of personality—"believed," as Marlow confesses, "where I had already ceased to doubt." "Worn and clouded," "overcome by a profound and helpless fatigue," Marlow cannot trust or enjoy or even acknowledge his own "special meaning." It seems to him, indeed, that he has no particularity or power, that he is cold at his core, stark, sterile, deeply and sadly insincere. He remarks:

> As to me, I have no imagination. . . . I felt I had done
> nothing. And what is it that I had wished to do? I am not
> sure now. . . . I remained strangely unenlightened. I was
> no longer young enough to behold at every turn the mag-
> nificence that besets our insignificant footsteps. . . . After
> all, what did *I* know? (Conrad's emphasis)

Marlow fears, this is to say, that because he has risked nothing and
understood nothing, he has achieved nothing. He fears that by sub-
stituting his tepid "ideal of conduct" for the primal exigencies of free
experience, his "sheltering conception of light and order" for the
threatening hazards of absolute personality, he has, like Brierly, "almost cheated his life of its legitimate terrors." (It is important to
remark the fact that Marlow never underestimates the price which
Jim pays for his splendid authenticity.) Perhaps—and only perhaps—
Marlow may be thought to be a more reliable man than Jim. But he
seems to himself less actual than his friends, less authentic in his
sensation of existence. (At one point in his narrative Marlow directly
acknowledges his inferiority to Jim. "I was the irreproachable man,"
he remarks, "but [Jim's] selfishness had a higher origin, a more lofty
aim.") He never has abandoned a sinking ship; but he has abandoned, as he believes, the exalted project and exacting pleasures of a
life that is genuinely human.
   It is for this reason that by the end of his narrative Marlow
acknowledges Jim not only as a friend but as a savior of sorts.

> [Jim] had startled me out of a dream of wandering through
> empty spaces whose immensity had harassed my soul and
> exhausted my body. . . . I felt a gratitude, an affection, for
> that straggler whose eyes had singled me out, keeping my
> place in the ranks of an insignificant multitude. How little
> that was to boast of, after all!

Considered from this point of view, Jim in his "sheer truthfulness"
legitimizes not only his own existence but Marlow's as well. "I'd lost
all confidence in myself," Marlow confesses. If Jim cannot return his
older friend to his happily exploded sense of gratitude and ease, he
can stir and excite him, permit him access to significance and particularity. It seems to the "harassed" and "exhausted" Marlow a magnificent gift.

V

It is precisely from this point, though, that one feels there to be something computational about Marlow's relationship with Jim, a subtle taint of manipulation and use where once, perhaps, there had been simple generosity. As their intimacy progresses, that is, Marlow appears to divine in Jim not a man in need of aid but a system of help for his own pain, an instrument of recovery from his own instinction of vapidity and squalor.

At the very least there develops an increasingly co-optative tone about Marlow's responses to Jim. After all, he begins his account of their association by remarking that originally he had felt merely an "interest" in Jim, a gratuitous "curiosity" about his character. Soon, though, the quality of Marlow's "interest" suggests a more extreme investment, an indelicate hint of usurpation in place of that initial spontaneous sympathy. Thus, as he meets with Stein he not entirely ironically refers to Jim as both a "toy"—"one of those flat wooden figures that are worked by a string"—and "a specimen." (Marlow is capable of yet less pleasant attitudes toward other men. About the dying Brown, for example, he remarks: "I had to bear the sunken glare of his fierce crow-footed eyes if I wanted to know; and so I bore it." Later he adds: "He died during the night, I believe, but by that time I had nothing more to learn." Certain of his impulses about Jim are disturbing enough, to be sure. Marlow reports, for instance, that he and Stein "avoided pronouncing Jim's name as though we had tried to keep flesh and blood out of our discussion, or he were nothing but an erring spirit, a suffering and nameless shade.") And in a moment of radical self-exposure he goes on to define the full reach of his acquisitive, of his virtually taxonomic, interest in his "distinct" and "touching" friend:

> I could see in his glance darted into the night all his inner being carried on, projected headlong. . . . [Jim] began to pace the room, reminding me by the set of his shoulders, the turn of his head, the headlong and uneven stride, of that night when he had paced thus, confessing, explaining—what you will—but, in the last instance, living—living before me.

In the end, then, Jim so attracts and compels Marlow because Marlow imagines that he actually can *attach* himself to Jim, that he can seize upon Jim's emotive authenticity and make part of it his own. "The views he let [Marlow] have of himself," of his splendidly actual "inner being," seem to Marlow so redolent with expressiveness, sincerity, and reality that he thinks to affiliate himself with their quality, to link himself by sympathy—if not by mere proximity—with his friend's heroic genuineness.

VI

The essential device and gesture of this interesting strategy is the narrative act itself. For Marlow believes that it is principally by organizing, interpreting, and recording Jim's experience that he can associate himself with it. If, that is, it be Jim who actually makes "the conquest of love, honour, men's confidence," it is Marlow who perceives that fact and publicizes its implications. If it be Jim, the pioneering partner, who lives in "unconscious subtlety," it is Marlow who makes his subtlety usable by raising it to vibrant consciousness. It seems to Marlow, therefore, that his narrative simultaneously permits Jim to claim the full significance and quality of his "greatness" and permits Marlow himself to become coadjutant with it. It seems to Marlow that by comprehending and advertising Jim's adventure he at once salvages his partner's delicacy from obscurity and meaninglessness and establishes a vantage point for his own.

It is for this reason that, in one of the most important passages in Conrad's early fiction, Marlow feels able to assert, "[Jim's] is a victory in which I had taken my part." He goes on to declare:

> I am telling you so much about my own instinctive feel-
> ings and bemused reflections because there remains so little
> to be told of him. He existed for me, and after all it is only
> through me that he exists for you. I've led him out by the
> hand; I have paraded him before you.

(It is possible to suggest that Marlow uses the preposition "for" in a curious way here. It seems to me that at least in part he intends to suggest that Jim conducts his life on *behalf* of Marlow—that he "existed" for the sake of enlivening Marlow's "exhausted" sensibility. If this be so, Marlow should seem to possess at once a more selfish and a more social imagination than any other character in literature.) "I", "I've," "I"; "my," "me," "me." The man who had demeaned himself as illegitimate and insignificant appears to have developed a use for—and an interest in—his "own instinctive feelings and bemused reflections." The man who had loathed and reviled himself seems to have discovered a lovely potential in the contemplative devices of his "exhausted" character, a way of making himself suppose, as had Jim, that his own quietistic "existence is necessary—you see, absolutely necessary—to another person."

The narrative act, then, seems to Marlow both to establish and to justify his existence. (I have used Conrad's personal vocabulary deliberately: for Marlow's achievement of certitude and serenity obviously establishes the ground for Conrad's own.) Certainly his recital promises to preserve hislife's most intense, as one might say, his most "romantic" experience. For it has been in his association with Jim that, as he remarks, the most "tremulous, subdued, and impassioned note . . . had come in [his] way"; it has been in his association with Jim that Marlow most has felt himself to possess "a special meaning," to be in his own right "touched" and "wonderful." By narrating Lord Jim, by describing his partner's story and his own "part" in it, Marlow finds himself able to regain and to perpetuate that sensation of authority, that movement of personality, which his intimacy with Jim had provoked autonomously. By reconstructing his cherished past as an organized narrative Marlow finds himself able to resurrect "the whole real thing" which otherwise should have "left behind the detailed and amazing impression of a dream." By arresting in language the moments of his own "greatness" he rescues for use in the present "the sounds, the visions, the very savour of the past." By describing his association with Jim as a composed and ordered tale Marlow recovers in both a semantic and an emotional context his entire consciousness of its quality, reproduces in both language and sensation its bold and not again *experientially* discoverable "truthfulness." (Marlow had believed in Patusan, it will be recalled, that one could not achieve so much as this. Jewel's voice, he remarked then, "had the power to drive me out of my conception of existence, out of that shelter each of us makes for himself to creep under in moments of danger, as a tortoise withdraws within its shell. . . . But still—it was only a moment: I went back into my shell directly. One *must*—don't you know?" [Conrad's emphasis]. Perhaps one must "withdraw" in this way. But by narrating the events of *Lord Jim* Marlow produces a way repeatedly to perform that expansion—that creation—of himself which he had discovered in

Patusan.) "I can easily picture [Jim] to myself," he reports. "I remember the smallest details; . . . I can testify."

VII

More than personal "testimony," though, is at issue in this ambitious enterprise. For Marlow's idea of himself is almost wholly at the mercy of his listeners—of his own certifying partners. Should he be unable to make his audience perceive his experience with Jim in its full particularity and force, he cannot, as he believes, entirely reclaim it—nor feel it to be established in perfect signification and durability. So it is that, in another of the novel's important moments, he remarks of his impressions in Patusan:

> All I had lately seen, all I had heard, and the very human speech itself, seemed to have passed away out of existence, living only for a while longer in my memory, as though I had been the last of mankind. . . . This was, indeed, one of the lost, forgotten, unknown places of the earth; I had looked under its obscure surface; and I felt that when tomorrow I had left it for ever, it would slip out of existence, to live only in my memory till I myself passed into oblivion. I have that feeling about me now; perhaps it is that feeling which has incited me to tell you the story, to try to hand over to you, as it were, its very existence, its reality—the truth disclosed in a moment of illusion.

Obviously Marlow refers here less to Patusan or his responses to Patusan than to his character itself: as I have remarked, it is chiefly his own sensibility which Marlow finds "one of the lost, forgotten, unknown places of the earth." By describing "the story" of his decisive experience, though, by treating his life as a tellable tale, Marlow hopes to hold, as it were to entrust to others, his character's "very existence, its reality." In this sense, perhaps, he imagines that he can make of "a moment of illusion" a lifetime—or more—of tangible, irrefutable "truth."

If this be a brave strategy, it is as well a deeply dangerous one. As Marlow acknowledges, he has tried "to hand over" to his audience the foundation of his identity. Should he fail to earn the belief and trust of his listeners he shall risk not merely their boredom but his own collapse as an organized and sensible personality. It is for this reason that Marlow feels there to be so much at stake in his uses of language. Words have no arcane function for this extraordinary seaman because, as I have suggested, at stake for Marlow in his power to make others understand his communications is nothing less than his power to be. No wonder, then, he is so frantic after precision of expression, literalness of effect:

> I am trying to interpret for you into slow speech the instantaneous effect of visual impressions. . . . All this, as I've warned you, gets dwarfed in the telling. I can't with mere words convey to you the impression. . . . This is my impression and it is all I can give you. . . . Try as I may for the *success* of this yarn I am missing innumerable shades— they were so fine, so difficult to render in colourless words . . . I have given up expecting those last words, whose ring, if they could only be pronounced, would shake both heaven and earth. (my emphasis)

"The *success* of this yarn." Unless he can describe exactly the full nuance of his moments of former feeling, Marlow feels that he must lose them forever—and so lose himself. As he puts the matter, "Should I let [my life with Jim] slip away into the darkness I would never forgive myself." (Marlow's anxiety is compounded by the fact that he cannot trust fully to the responsiveness of his audience. He remarks at one point in the narrative: " 'Frankly, it is not my words that I mistrust but your minds. I could be eloquent were I not afraid that you fellows had starved your imaginations to feed your bodies.' " His concern seems well-founded; he is forced to write to his unnamed correspondent: "You alone have showed an interest in [Jim] that survived the telling of his story." Marlow is not always convinced, though, of the legitimacy of language; " 'for words also,' " he once declares, " 'belong to the sheltering conception of light and order which is our refuge' " from the burdens of full authenticity.)

Perhaps, then, Marlow, unlike Jim, cannot "dare" to say that he has become "satisfied . . . nearly." His satisfaction, after all, is still at issue as he leaves the novel and must again be placed at issue each time that he tells his story. Yet, it seems to me that in *Lord Jim* Marlow does achieve a "victory," or at least a "greatness," akin to his partner's "extraordinary success." For Marlow, too, has had the courage and skill to attempt an accommodation with the universe and with himself. Like Jim, Marlow refuses to be "not worth having." Like Jim, Marlow undertakes "to prove his power in another way" from that given to most men, and thus to "conquer the fatal destiny itself" of his own self-loathing. At the least, as he remarks about Jim, Marlow's seemingly depleted "spirit seemed to rise above the ruins of his existence." And why should it not? Out of materials far less promising than even his partner's, he manages to create for himself an approach to "that full utterance which," as he declares, "through all our stammerings is of course our only and abiding intention."

In Marlow's case that utterance, if not full, seems fully serviceable. "My information was fragmentary," he exults, "but I've fitted the pieces together, and there is enough to make an intelligible picture." This is to say that in his inspired discovery of the uses of language Marlow assembles not simply a novel but "an intelligible picture" of a personality. By narrating *Lord Jim* he collects from among all the incoherence of his unpleasure and unbeing "something of me—the best." Out of the most meager and fragmented resources and with the offered assistance of no one Marlow shapes himself as a man whom he can bear to be. For the first time in his life he frees himself from the bleak oppressiveness of the outer world and the sad ravages of his own aberrant psychology. Perhaps he cannot join that community discovered by other novelists' characters, the community of the fully peaceful and the fully free. No one in Conrad's fiction, though, is permitted to achieve quite so much as this.

VIII

Obviously at work here for Conrad, who, after all, is Marlow's narrator, is a crucial gesture of *self*-reconciliation: it has been my point in this study that what Marlow does in literature Conrad hoped to do in life, that what Marlow achieves in fiction Conrad wished to achieve as a maker of fiction. Just as Marlow recovers from his fear that he has no character by producing a linguistic or a narrative self, so Conrad, by telling Marlow's tale, by attaching himself to Marlow as Marlow attaches himself to Jim, may be thought at last to have produced and secured a serviceable personality of his own. At the least Conrad may be said to have established in *Lord Jim*—together with his earlier novels—an explanation of his life's chief ambition and procedure. For if he no more than Marlow or Jim could achieve in his novels "that full utterance" or "those last words," he did produce for his own use the terms of that external justification for which he so long had searched. " 'I don't want to excuse myself,' " he has Jim say, " 'but I would like to explain—I would like somebody to understand—somebody—one person at least! You! Why not you?' "

By 1900, to be understood by "somebody"—by us, indeed—proposed itself to Conrad as both an acceptable apparatus of character and an acceptable system of sanction. The twin impulses—to establish "an intelligible picture" of himself and to legitimize the picture by his readers' comprehension of its integuments—for the rest of his life offered itself to Conrad as a bulwark against his "awful vision" and a defense against his mind's "unreasonable forces." Thus, as he began the second era of his career as a novelist Conrad felt able to say, in however ironic a way, that like Marlow and Jim he, too, was "satisfied . . . nearly." To Garnett, who always had understood something of his anxiety and sorrow, he wrote:

> I admit I stood [in *Lord Jim*] for a great triumph and I have only succeeded in giving myself utterly away. Nobody'll see it, but you have detected me falling back into my lump of clay I had been lugging up from the bottom of the pit, with the idea of breathing big life into it. And all I have done was to let it fall with a silly crash. . . .
>
> I've been satanically ambitious but there's nothing of a devil in me, worse luck. The *Outcast* is a heap of sand, the *Nigger* a splash of water, *Jim* a lump of clay. A stone, I suppose, will be my next gift to the impatient mankind—before I get drowned in mud to which even my supreme struggles won't give a simulacrum of life. Poor mankind! Drop a tear for it—but look how infinitely more pathetic I am! This pathos is a kind of triumph no criticism can touch. Like the philosopher who crowed at the Universe I shall know when I am utterly squashed. This time I am only very bruised, very sore, very humiliated.
>
> This is the effect of the book upon me; the intimate and personal effect. Humiliation. Not extinction. Not yet. All of you stand by me so nobly that I must still exist.

Anyone who reads widely in Conrad's correspondence will recognize the letter's excitement and hope. The self-mockery notwithstanding—Conrad never freed himself from *that* idiom—the letter is all alive with a sense of opportunity and renewal almost unique for him. "Not extinction. Not yet." Far from it: during the next ten years of his life Conrad worked with the greatest power of his life. (Perhaps, like Jim, he "could no more stop telling now than he could have stopped living by the mere exertion of his will.") And if he could not live during that decade in anything like perfect equanimity and repose, he did manage largely to preserve "the belief in himself snatched from the fire," "the big life" he had breathed into "the lump of clay" which had been himself. Like the lights flickering from the deserted *Patna,* he sent into the world volume after volume of his continuing "simulacrum of life," as if to say to more established men, " 'I am here—still here.' " As he remarks in *Lord Jim,* "What more can . . . the most forsaken of human beings say?"

Conrad's personal achievement in *Lord Jim* was as "immense," then, as that of his characters. As he has Marlow say of Jim, he created for himself in the novel "a seal of success upon his words, . . . conquered ground for the soles of his feet, [gained] the blind trust of men." The edifice which Conrad erected in his spectacularly difficult way, this "simulacrum of life," doubtless was less one of personality than of performance. But this was his courage: like Marlow, like Jim, he was willing to have his character at any hazard, to chance his whole identity upon his own continuing authority as an author and upon our intelligence as readers. (Conrad always was frank about both the totality of his risk and its desperate psychic cost. The letters which I have cited and his lifelong bouts with temper, self-loathing, illness, and doubt comprise a terrible testimony to the constancy of his incertitude and worry.) In this regard one dares say that no other novelist ever can have invested so much in his work as Conrad habitually did in his. Certainly no other novelist can have been more at the mercy of—or more empowered by—his sovereignty with language. The fullest measure of Conrad's success with this appalling, albeit self-defined, burden is the fact that against all odds he remained sane. Or perhaps it is rather the fact that after completing *Lord Jim* he for the most part ceased to write covert autobiography of the kind I have tried to define in this study; the fact that Conrad felt released enough by having written fiction about himself to extend his attention more directly to the psychology and the society of others.

This is to say that after writing *Lord Jim* Conrad at last became able to satisfy Thaddeus Bobrowski's most difficult injunction.

"From the blending of the blood in [the] two excellent races in your worthy person," Bobrowski had written to Conrad in 1880, "should spring a character whose endurance and wise enterprise will cause the whole world to be astonished!" (Baines). As, fifty years after his death, Conrad increasingly seems to us our century's most important novelist, I think it inevitable that we shall learn to regard him as our most interesting as well. It is true that we are not yet so "astonished" by Conrad's "endurance and wise enterprise" as we ought to be. But as we are led by the quality of the fictions which those energies produced to investigate the personality which controlled them, we cannot fail to become excited by the extremity of Conrad's will to identify and to justify himself. To be sure, an author's private struggle for coherence and peace—the century's struggle—is not a traditional subject for criticism. In Conrad's case, though, as his guardian implied before the fact, the literature is otherwise incomprehensible.

Lord Jim and the Pear Tree Caper

D. M. Halperin

"Every art and every inquiry—and, similarly, every act and choice—seems to aim at some good; therefore, the good has quite properly been declared to be that at which all things aim": so begins Aristotle's *Nicomachean Ethics*. This well-nigh incontrovertible statement has from time to time been called into question by men whose experience of life and of themselves has lacked the serenity and self-assurance which appears to have characterized Aristotle's outlook.

The second book of Augustine's *Confessions* is largely devoted to the so-called "Pear Tree Caper." When Augustine was sixteen, he was obliged to live at home for a year while his father scraped together the necessary funds for his higher education at Carthage. Time weighed heavily on the young Augustine. One night, he and a group of his comrades invaded a neighbor's orchard and plundered a pear tree; thirty years later Augustine dissects this act with horror and loathing. The Pear Tree Caper, often pointed to as an example of Augustine's capacity for neurotic obsession, takes on in fact a crucial significance as a disturbing ethical conundrum.

Augustine cannot account for his crime. He was not hungry or poor, the pears were not particularly attractive in themselves, and better ones were available to Augustine at home. He tasted them only to fling them at swine. Not spurred on by love of danger, he did not aim at the exercise of a faculty which could later be turned to good purpose. Although he thrilled to the sin and to his sense of sin, Augustine did not steal for the sake of pleasure, since pleasure (in

From *American Notes and Queries* 14, no. 8 (April 1976). © 1976 by Erasmus Press.

Augustine's classical framework) is the enjoyment of a good and the theft of pears aimed at no good whatsoever. Augustine suggests that he may have acted from a desire to manifest his power, dignity, and an (illusory) freedom, but he finds this solution far from satisfactory. He also dismisses as insufficient the need for companionship and self-expression. Augustine is stumped. He experienced a mysterious and irresistible attraction that led to the commission of a gratuitous crime.

The Pear Tree Caper is incomprehensible within the categories of traditional ethics. It constitutes an *unmotivated act*. It gives the lie to Augustine's classical conception of evil (the substitution of a lesser good for a greater good) and represents man's inexplicable tendency towards annihilation. Its importance for Augustine's thought is clear: if man cannot understand himself, then neither can he save himself; left to his own devices, he is powerless to avoid sin. The very trivial and commonplace nature of the Pear Tree Caper only adds to its horror—it is shown to be not the exception but the rule. This celebrated incident from Augustine's biography argues with unforgettable power that the full consequences of the Fall are to be sought in the unfathomable darkness of the human heart.

Joseph Conrad's early stories, especially "Karain" and "Lagoon," demonstrate a concern with precisely the same phenomenon: the unaccountable act. Like Augustine, Conrad sets forth the issue in the most stark and frightening manner, focusing on what Albert Guerard has called "the conscientious man's impulsive, involuntary crime of betrayal."

Conrad accords this theme its most memorable treatment in his novel *Lord Jim*. Jim's "leap," his sudden act of cowardice, is entirely incomprehensible in the context of his personality. Jim may be a romantic and an egoist, but he is (as Marlow insists over and over again) "one of us": a man fashioned for a position of responsibility and trust. He is endowed with extraordinary courage, strength, and endurance—qualities highly valued by Conrad. Jim's crime thus reveals the existence of hidden depths within the personality where the decision to act is formed below the reach of conscious will or thought. It marks out the limits of self-knowledge beyond which a man is incapable of understanding himself or predicting his own behavior. Jim's cowardice, like Augustine's theft of pears, betrays the inner darkness at the core of human personality.

It need not surprise us therefore that Conrad sees Jim's crime partly in Augustinian terms. A friend of Marlow's is moved to remark about Jim:

> Of course I guess there is something—some awful little scrape—which you know all about—but if I am sure that it is terribly heinous, I fancy one could manage to forgive it. For my part, I declare that I am unable to imagine him guilty of anything much worse than ROBBING AN ORCHARD. Is *it* much worse? Perhaps you ought to have told me; but it is such a long time since we both turned SAINTS that you may have forgotten we, too, had SINNED IN OUR TIME?

The allusion to the Pear Tree Caper may be unintentional; but, considering the numerous empirical similarities between Augustine's and Conrad's view of the human personality and of its "irrational residue," this passage may provide a clue to one of the literary sources of Conrad's imagination.

The Ending

Ian Watt

Critical discussion of the Patusan episode has largely concentrated on Jim's state of mind in three periods of the narrative: during Marlow's visit; at the time of his dealings with Gentleman Brown; and when the final catastrophe occurs. In all three cases Conrad's intentions have often been obscured by modern preconceptions.

Marlow's account of his month or so in Patusan is dominated by an atmosphere of foreboding. The enclosing jungle, the Stygian river, the general prevalence of dusk, obscurity, and shadow, compose a dark backdrop against which Jim, "white from head to foot," stands out in "total and utter isolation." Even Jim's three years of fame, Marlow says, took their "tone from the stillness and gloom of the land without a past, where his word was the one truth of every passing day."

Jim's own consciousness also has its sombre undercurrents; although he tells Marlow that he is "satisfied . . . nearly," he still yearns to "frame a message to the impeccable world." To some extent, therefore, one must agree with the judgment of many of the novel's best critics that Jim has not achieved "redemption" [Albert J. Guerard] or "atonement" [Robert E. Kuehn] in Patusan, nor "transcended the world of the *Patna*" [Tony Tanner]. But it is surely playing with loaded dice to apply such terms to *Lord Jim*. Neither the terms nor the assumptions underlying them would have been accepted as appropriate by Conrad, who firmly rejected the optimistic

From *Conrad in the Nineteenth Century*. © 1979 by the Regents of the University of California. University of California Press, 1979.

religious or transcendental assumptions which they imply. Conrad, like Marlow, is willing to settle for more relative and modest gains; and neither would expect much more than what has happened: that courage, work, and self-discipline have led Jim, not to apotheosis, but to feel "I am all right."

It is in any case far from clear what "atonement" or "redemption" might mean in the secular world of *Lord Jim*. There is no one to whom Jim can make reparation for his desertion of the *Patna*, and he himself was, and remains, its chief victim. It is true that Jim, very humanly, had earlier hoped that he might begin again "with a clean slate," but this was obviously unrealistic; as Marlow put it in the manuscript, "Once some potent event evokes before your eyes the invisible thing there is no way to make yourself blind again." On Patusan Jim faces the truth that none of his triumphs can ever wipe the slate clean; there is always, he says, "the bally thing at the back of my head." "The world outside," Jim confesses, "is enough to give me a fright . . . because I have not forgotten why I came here. Not yet!"

This inability to forget the *Patna*, however, will not seem to Jim's discredit to anyone who believes that the moral life depends, among other things, on treating our actions as in some sense permanent for ourselves and others. In any case, to wish otherwise would be to require Jim to accept the kind of celestial illusion on which the Intended relies in *Heart of Darkness*, and which, indeed, would have been needed to exorcise Jewel's continual terror that one day the outside world would rob her of Jim. Marlow knows very well that to kill such fears "you require . . . an enchanted and poisoned shaft dipped in a lie too subtle to be found on earth"; and to find that kind of deliverance, Marlow comments scornfully to his listeners, would be "An enterprise for a dream, my masters!"

The same ancient hunger for a magical transformation of reality has been at work in much of the psychological criticism of *Lord Jim*; it animates, for instance, such objections as that Jim fails to achieve full self-knowledge, that he is still "an outcast from himself . . . unable to recognize his own identity" [Dorothy Van Ghent] or that he continues to exist in the "mist of self-deception" [Guerard]. Here again there is evidence to support the charges; Marlow certainly says that Jim "was not clear to himself"; but he concedes that "I did not know so much more about myself," and also makes the wider judgment that "no man ever understands quite his own artful dodges to escape from the grim shadow of self-knowledge." Conrad's austere scepticism would probably have echoed Marlow's denials that complete self-knowledge is possible in this vale of tears; and the question therefore arises whether Jim, or indeed anyone, should be judged and found wanting by standards derived from the unsupported modern dogmas that full self-knowledge is possible and that it can deliver us from the ignominious fate of being what we are.

In general Conrad's novels suggest that he thought character was impervious to full comprehension; it was also nearly as intractable as circumstance, and equally unlikely to be transformed in accordance with our wishes. *Lord Jim* is not a *Bildungsroman,* and it treats character from two resolutely sceptical points of view. Conrad's presentation of Jim is sceptical in the impressionist way, because he is portrayed almost entirely through Marlow, who has no privileged knowledge of the "real" person such as an omniscient author might have claimed. Secondly, Conrad's portrayal is sceptical morally, because it does not show any large transformation of Jim's character. Jim, like everyone else, no doubt dreams of salvation, but he must settle for being seasoned.

At that more modest level of improvement, Marlow has cause to be delighted; but Jim's essential nature is unchanged: his way of thought, his naïve romanticism, his ingenuous and boy-scoutish devotion to the importance of his role, his moody self-preoccupation— all these components of the old Jim are still there on Patusan; all that has changed is that they are no longer disabling; all that has been transformed, as Marlow nicely puts it, is that now "there was a high seriousness in his stammerings."

For similar reasons it is surely a mistake to make too much of how Jim has lost his freedom and is in effect "possessed by this land of his dreams" [Tanner]. Jim has made his choice, and every choice has a price. All that can fairly be asked of him is that he should be clearsighted about the price; and this he surely is—taking his chance of drinking the rajah's coffee, which may be poisoned, making a fuss over disputes about turtles' eggs, and accepting all the other trivial annoyances of his daily routines. And in fact he is more than just satisfied with the result of his choice. "Now and then," Marlow reports, "a word, a sentence, would escape him that showed how deeply, how solemnly, he felt about that work which had given him the certitude of rehabilitation." Earlier, as a seaman, "the perfect love of the work," had "eluded him"; Jim has now found a form of this love: Marlow reports that "he seemed to love the land and the people," although he adds the qualification that he loved it "with a sort of fierce egoism, with a contemptuous tenderness."

The question is how seriously one must assess such reservations. Much has been made, for instance, of the damaging implications of Marlow's observation that "all his conquests, the trust, the fame, the friendships, the love—all these things that made him master had made him a captive, too." But this is not really a sign of Jim's failure; in the real world, such a captivity is surely an unanticipated but in practice inevitable result of assuming almost any responsibility— even that of literary criticism—seriously: the subjects are what they are, and make their own demands.

Many of the critics who take a severe view of Jim's failure to transform himself have centered their argument on his dealings with Gentleman Brown, the piratical ruffian who turns up in desperate straits and attempts to plunder Patusan. It has often been maintained that Jim is still psychologically crippled by an enduring sense of guilt, which leads him to identify unconsciously with Brown, and that this is why he lets Brown escape, thus bringing disaster upon himself and Patusan. The various versions of this view, first put forward by Gustav Morf, and widely accepted—by Albert Guerard, for instance—argue that Jim's error is due to the "paralyzing" and "immobilizing bond" brought about by his unconscious identification with Brown, that he "simply cannot resist the evil *because the evil is within himself.*"

Marlow certainly stresses the moral intensity of their confrontation. On Brown's side the motives are conscious and very obvious. Brown, we are told, "hated Jim at first sight," because he "seemed to belong to things he had in the very shaping of his life contemned and flouted." Jim provokes the ideological hatred of Brown, the lawless and cruel adventurer, because on Patusan Jim represents the established moral and social code; and on his deathbed Brown still exults in the thought that he had "paid out the stuck-up beggar." When he first meets Jim, Brown tries to establish that they are equals, not only as English seamen but as criminals; he assumes that they both had to escape from civilisation for discreditable reasons, and that they are both in Patusan only in quest of "pretty pickings."

As to Jim, he is certainly shaken when Brown implies that no one would immure himself in so isolated a spot unless he had something to hide, and he completely loses his self-possession when Brown asserts that if "it came to saving one's life in the dark, one didn't care who else went." So Jim's consciousness of his own failure may well have strengthened his wish to spare Brown's life; and he may even have identified with Brown to the extent that he thought that, like himself, Brown ought to be given another chance. Nevertheless, the weight of the evidence is far from supporting the view that Jim acted as he did out of guilt, whether conscious or unconscious, or that any other decision was possible.

When Gentleman Brown arrives with fourteen of his armed followers in a longboat, he is able to gain a foothold in Patusan only because Jim is absent, and the Rajah, Doramin, Dain Waris, and Jewel are unable to act in concert. They decide to await Jim's return, and by then only two choices remain: to give Brown "a clear road or else a clear fight." In a fight, Brown and his men would sell their lives dearly—they have already inflicted six casualties; and so Jim, who feels "responsible for every life in the land," decides to let Brown go. Realpolitik and local custom would no doubt dictate a more ruthless policy; but—quite apart from the fact that Brown is his countryman—everything that Jim stands for makes this alternative impossible: the extermination in cold blood of any human being—whatever their colour—would be morally offensive to anyone raised in the Western and Christian tradition, even if he were not, like Jim, the son of a parson; the decision, as Marlow sees it, ultimately involves Jim's "truth" as against the "creed" of Patusan. There is also a more idiosyncratic psychological reason: Jim has already shown that he prefers to take great risks rather than shed blood—as when he spared the three assassins who had been sent to kill him. In practical, in moral, and in psychological terms, then, Jim had no real alternative but to let Brown go, and whatever he may—consciously or unconsciously—have thought or felt about Brown could hardly have changed this.

Of course, Jim must take the blame, as anyone in charge must be blamed, when things turn out badly; it is quite normal for him to be criticised after the event. In objective terms, however, Jim was not even seriously imprudent. It is true that the catastrophe would not have occurred if Brown and his men had been disarmed; but Jim had originally made this stipulation, and gave it up only when Brown made it clear he would fight rather than surrender his arms. What finally happened, the massacre of Dain Waris and his men, could not have been predicted; no one could have foreseen the combination of what Marlow calls Brown's "almost inconceivable egotism," which impels him to an otherwise pointless act of murderous revenge, with the "intense hate" of Cornelius, who guides Brown to the backwater so that he can revenge himself indirectly against Jim, the man who has ousted him as Stein's representative.

There is, then, no reason to believe that Jim must have let Brown go out of guilt; but the question of guilt has a larger importance in the interpretation of Jim's character and fate. From the very beginning Jim puzzles and annoys Marlow largely because he apparently feels no guilt at having transgressed the mariner's code; what really matters to Jim is his personal failure to live up to his ego-ideal; and what he cannot bear is to face those who think that his real character is defined by his desertion of the *Patna*. Against such people Jim has only two reactions: to fight, or to blush. We see both reactions succeeding each other on his first meeting with Marlow: when Jim realises his mistake about the yellow cur, he is foiled of his unconscious need to relieve his feelings by giving Marlow "that hammering he was going to give me for rehabilitation"; instead, he blushes, and so deeply that "his ears became intensely crimson." Similarly, at the thoughts provoked by Brown's first question—"What made you come here?"—Jim gets "very red in the face."

In both cases Jim's blushing is surely a sign not of guilt, but of shame. The nature of the distinction remains moderately obscure, partly because the word "guilt" is used in so many different ways; but it is usually agreed that shame is much more directly connected than guilt with the individual's failure to live up to his own ideal conception of himself. As Gerhart Piers puts it in his psychoanalytic treatment of the distinction: "Whereas guilt is generated whenever a boundary (set by the Super-Ego) is touched or transgressed, shame occurs when a goal (presented by the Ego-Ideal) is not being reached. It thus indicates a real 'shortcoming.' Guilt anxiety accompanies transgression; shame, failure" (Gerhart Piers and Milton B. Singer, *Shame and Guilt: A Psychoanalytic and a Cultural Study*). Marlow characteristically judges Jim on the basis of guilt: "The idea obtrudes itself," Marlow comments, "that he made so much of his disgrace while it is the guilt alone that matters." The case of Brierly establishes the contrast. Brierly characteristically sees Jim primarily as a "disgrace" because his basic standards of judgment for himself and others are based on shame; and it is the thought of possibly falling short of his own ideal, not of transgression as such, which drives him to suicide.

The wider psychological implications of shame have been suggested by Max Scheler in terms which recall Stein's diagnosis of Jim. Scheler sees the origin of shame in the discrepancy between the individual's inward conception of himself and how his appearance and acts seem to others. As the most famous example of this disparity between man as a conscious spiritual being and man as an unreflective animal, Scheler cites the shame of Adam and Eve after the fall (*La Pudeur,* trans. M. Dupuy). For Jim the equivalent crisis of self-knowledge presumably came after his jump from the *Patna;* and his intense suffering, as Stein saw, arose from his realisation of the disjunction between essence and existence, between his dreams and his act.

To return to Jim's motives with Gentleman Brown, it should be pointed out that Marlow does not see guilt as an explanation. When he emphasises Brown's "sickening suggestion of common guilt," he is clearly referring to guilt in its sense of culpability for crime; and in any case Marlow emphasises that Brown didn't as he thought, "turn Jim's soul inside out," because it was, Marlow affirms, "so utterly out of his reach."

If we seek to explain the causes of the widespread assumption that Jim's decision to let Brown go, and therefore his death, were the product of his guilty identification with Brown, we must surely find them, not in the text, but in that strange Freudian mutation of the doctrine of original sin, which has now established as an *a priori* postulate that all errors are the result of unconscious guilt. This convenient moral melodrama enables us to retain two comforting beliefs: that the world is just; and that despite all contrary appearances people who suffer have only themselves to blame. These doctrines give us the pleasurable duty, as soon as we see Jim make a fateful error, to discover discreditable unconscious motives which prove that Jim deserved to be punished. Dorothy Van Ghent, for instance, compares the fates of Jim and Oedipus, and asks the question, "Is one guilty for circumstances?" Through the privileged immunity to the complexities of other people's circumstances which is granted by a modern psychology, we can return the unhesitating verdict of "Guilty."

On hearing that Brown has massacred Dain Waris and his followers, Jim's first thought is to avenge their death: but when Tamb' Itam says that the people of Patusan have turned against him, Jim realises that this is out of the question. Three possible courses of action remain. If Jim is to keep Jewel and his followers with him, he must, like Brown, either fight or run. Both are hazardous; neither would benefit Patusan; fighting would cause much bloodshed; and escape might be a repetition of *Patna*. Jim's few, and rather oracular, answers to Jewel and Tamb' Itam make it clear that he does not choose to fight because "I have no life," and so "There is nothing to fight for." As for escape, Marlow thinks that Jim soon resolved that "the dark powers should not rob him twice of his peace."

The third possible course of action is to go to Doramin, and Marlow assumes that Jim decided on this almost at once; he would "defy the disaster in the only way it occurred to him such a disaster could be defied," and "conquer the fatal destiny itself." In making his choice Jim must have known that Doramin would want a life for a life—Jim's blood for that of his son, Dain Waris; and so Jim is in effect choosing a form of suicide. The mood in which Jim silently makes up his mind certainly suggests a defeated apathy somewhat similar to that which immobilised him on the *Patna,* and Marlow's comment on Jim's frame of mind then seems equally appropriate now: "The desire of peace waxes stronger as hope declines, till at last it conquers the very desire of life." In the lifeboat Jim had wished for death partly out of revulsion from the defiling contact of the three other officers; and Cornelius and Brown are very like them in that they take the lowest possible view of life as egotistical survival. They represent what Tony Tanner has called the beetle view of the world; on this analogy, Jim's final choice is that of a butterfly who wants to fly above the earthbound corruption which once again has fouled his life.

Conrad, however, knew very well that a particular action could be psychologically complex and yet inevitable: Marlow's lie to the Intended is an example. Jim's mood of defeated self-withdrawal during his last hours need not in itself, therefore, invalidate the view that he really had very little choice except to go to Doramin; and it is surely Marlow's—and Conrad's—intention to make us feel that Jim's decision was inevitable. After all, it conforms to Jim's most explicit obligation, his formal promise to the people of Patusan that "he was ready to answer with his life for any harm that should come to them if the white men with beards were allowed to retire." Great harm has come, and what Marlow calls "the sheer truthfulness of his last three years of life," that same truthfulness which had swayed Jim's people when he argued them into letting Brown go, now demands that Jim should be ready to keep his word and thus affirm his solidarity with those who had trusted him.

On the basis of its first four chapters, we would expect *Lord Jim* to be about the follies and the dangers of the simple human impulse to daydream about flattering romantic adventures. In his youth Conrad had shared the dream; but he began his career as a writer under something like the standard modern prescription—when fearful of self-exposure, take cover in irony: and so *Lord Jim* opens with a critical and sardonic view of its hero and his self-indulgent dreams. This negative attitude is increasingly qualified by sympathy during Marlow's narrative, but it does not wholly disappear until the Stein episode. There Jim is elevated to an unexpected metaphysical dignity; to have failed as an adventure-story hero is to become a symbol of the romantic world-view. On Patusan a paradoxical reversal occurs, and Jim becomes a genuine hero of romance. It is as though, having demonstrated that he knew the case against adventurous aspirations, Conrad had decided to try out a new fictional hypothesis. In the apt terms of Jean-Jacques Mayoux, "A romantic finds his bearings again in a romantic situation; a devotee of unreality is at last at ease in an unreal and fabulous world where his imaginings precede and create the events instead of being surprised by them (*Vivants piliers*).

Conrad's reversal of his original fictional assumptions no doubt reflects a continuing personal irresolution. If *Lord Jim* is the most romantic of Conrad's works, it may be because he began it as a sad and affectionate farewell to an earlier self, but then discovered that the parting would be too painful unless he first granted that romantic self some of the satisfactions it had dreamed of long ago. This changed aim may have helped to impel the last part of *Lord Jim* towards other formal literary models, and in particular towards the very different traditions of romance and tragedy; both had been intermittently suggested earlier, but in Patusan romance becomes the dominant spirit until that of tragedy partly displaces it at the end.

Much of the action, the setting, the characters and the symbolism of Patusan suggest fable, fairy tale, and especially medieval romance. In Patusan, where "Romance had singled Jim for its own," the land and its people "exist as if under an enchanter's wand." Like a wandering knight, Jim arrives in an enchanted kingdom and there triumphs over incredible odds to deliver the people from their oppressors, notably Sherif Ali and his "infernal crew." In addition, just as his mentor Stein had been rewarded for his "innumerable exploits" with the hand of a princess, so Jim wins the hand of a persecuted maiden, Jewel; they come together, we are told, "under the shadow of a life's disaster, like knight and maiden meeting to exchange vows amongst haunted ruins."

It can hardly be denied that such conventional elements of romance necessarily involve a marked falling off from the moral and dramatic intensity of the first part of *Lord Jim;* and this led F. R. Leavis to place *Lord Jim* among Conrad's minor works on the ground that "the romance that follows" the *Patna* episodes, "though plausibly offered as a continued exhibition of Jim's case, has no inevitability as that." The continuity between Jim of the *Patna* and Tuan Jim of Patusan is certainly not one of complete inevitability. On the other hand, Conrad is remarkably successful in adjusting the formulae of romance to his very different fictional premises. This is evident, for instance, in the ingenuity with which the silver ring is used to bring about an ironic variation on the folk-tale motif of the poisoned gift, and thus to symbolise the transition from Jim's moment of glory to his fatal destiny.

The ring was given to Stein by Doramin, his old "war-comrade," as a token of "eternal friendship." Stein gives it to Jim as his introduction to Doramin; and soon after his arrival in Patusan, when Jim is being pursued by his enemies, the ring becomes the magic emblem which causes Doramin to save his life and set him on the road of triumph. After that, however, the ring plays a less auspicious role. Jim sends it by messenger to Dain to vouch for his order that Brown be allowed safe-passage to the sea; it is then returned to Doramin with Dain's corpse; and the cycle of friendship and trust comes to an end when, as he rises to shoot Jim, the ring falls from Doramin's lap and rolls against Jim's foot. The talisman which had first "opened . . . the door of fame, love, and success" to Jim, now closes it forever.

This symbolic reversal is complemented by another. Doramin owns a pair of huge ebony and silver flintlock pistols which Stein gave him long ago in return for the ring. Stein, in turn, had received the pistols from his early benefactor in the Celebes, a Scot called Alexander M'Neil; and it is out of gratitude to him that Stein plans the reciprocal gesture of adopting a Briton, if not a Scot, and decides to make Jim his heir. The continuity of this cycle of trust and friendship is also broken when Doramin avenges the death of his only son; he does it by shooting Stein's adopted son with the gift his old friend had given him to seal their friendship.

Jim's romantic imagination has made him what he is; it has

brought him to Patusan; and there his destiny is consummated with something of the spare and sudden brevity of Greek tragedy. This destiny, however, has been foreshadowed throughout the novel. The conflict between Jim and the world can never be appeased or resolved; and the unyielding determination with which he confronts it gives Jim something of the moral grandeur of the tragic hero. As Marlow puts it, Jim becomes an "individual in the forefront of his kind," because his problem is one where "the obscure truth involved" seems "momentous enough to affect mankind's conception of itself."

In this respect also Patusan constitutes, not a new departure, but a concluding thematic variation./Jim thinks that he can at last be wholly isolated from the past; but in fact the *Patna* not only robs him of any inner peace, but also separates him from Patusan.) No one there can understand Jim: neither his adoptive family—Doramin and his wife—nor his friend, Dain Waris, knows his secret; and when Jim tells Jewel the story of the *Patna,* "she did not believe him." Jewel can only see the determining event of Jim's life as "an inexplicable and incomprehensible conspiracy to keep her for ever in the dark"; and when she asks him—"Has it got a face and a voice—this calamity?," Marlow finally realises that, despite the touching closeness of Jim and Jewel, their unhappy pasts will always keep them apart, and that therefore "their two benighted lives" must be irremediably "tragic."

Jim cannot possibly reconcile all the just claims upon him. It is this intractability of moral circumstance which goes far to justify Robert B. Heilman's claim that "Jim is that rare creature in English fiction—the tragic hero" (Introduction, Rinehart edition of *Lord Jim*). Several other critics, including Dorothy Van Ghent, have also considered him in this light, although usually to arrive at a qualified dissent.

The problem of whether we should see *Lord Jim* as tragedy is largely a matter of what we understand by the term. If, following the common critical view, we take as our main criterion for tragedy the hero's achievement of self-knowledge, Jim does not qualify. Heilman, it is true, speaks of Jim's having to go through "the tragic course of knowing himself and thus learning the way to salvation"; but convincing evidence of Jim's final moral maturity is surely far to seek. Marlow comments during his Patusan visit that "It's extraordinary how very few signs of wear he showed"; and what continues to make Jim attractive is largely his youthful surface of imperviousness to fortune's frown. In any case, Marlow's most explicit judgment on the issue of Jim's self-knowledge runs completely counter to Heilman's view: Jim, Marlow says, "was overwhelmed by his own personality—the gift of that destiny which he had done his best to master."

To postulate self-knowledge as a criterion of tragedy, however, may be yet another of the modern secularised versions of the consolations which religion offers in the face of suffering, waste, and evil. Certainly Heilman's assumption that self-knowledge leads to "salvation" might be taken as confirmation of this, and so might Dorothy Van Ghent's argument that what distinguishes Jim's death from the "atonement" of the exile of Orestes or Oedipus is that the expiation of Jim's blood-guilt brings about not the "restoration" but the "destruction" of "community health." Much could be said in general against the Hegelian theory that tragedy is socially reconstructive; but even if it were true of Greek tragedy, it is surely evident that both the form and the substance of *Lord Jim* take a very different view of the relation between society and the individual. To adopt Van Ghent's terminology, *Lord Jim,* like the modern novel in general, assumes, "the disintegration" of those very "moral bonds between men," which in classical tragedy are assumed to be the world's normative order.

In any case all the evidence suggests that the various Christian, Hegelian or Marxist theoretical systems which present suffering, conflict, or death as necessary parts of some promised transcendental recompense or dialectical reconciliation were, or would have been, completely alien to Conrad's way of looking at the world. That at one moment Marlow sees a "terrifying logic" in the operation of Jim's destiny does not mean he sees it as part of an ultimately just or moral process; on the contrary, as Marlow suggests in connection with the *Patna* episode, Jim's fate may be as meaningless, accidental, and "devoid of importance as the flooding of an ant-heap." Such a bleak perspective would not necessarily discount the view that *Lord Jim* is much closer to tragedy than most novels; but it would have to be tragic in other meanings of the term.

Another more archaic and less moralistic view of tragedy sees it primarily as the expression of humanity's awed astonishment at the works of fate, and more especially at its remorseless dealings with individuals who are far above the common run, not only in their position and achievements, but in the resolution with which they confront suffering and death. Such a reaction is expressed by one of the men of Patusan at the fate of Dain Waris: he is "struck with a great awe and wonder at the 'suddenness of men's fate, which hangs over their heads like a cloud charged with thunder.' " This feeling is surely the essence of Marlow's own reaction to Jim's destiny; and Conrad probably intended Jim's last act to leave the reader with a sense not of pity but of a half-comprehending yet dazzled admiration very similar to the awe which the death of the tragic hero inspires.

Many other views of tragedy see it not as the resolution but as the culmination of conflict. Schopenhauer, for instance, saw the "purpose" of tragedy as "the description of the terrible side of life . . . the wretchedness and misery of mankind, the triumph of wickedness, the scornful mastery of chance, and the irretrievable fall of the just and the innocent." Jim's state of mind before going to Doramin is consistent with Schopenhauer's view of the tragic protagonist who eventually refuses to be deceived by "the phenomenon, the veil of Maya," and whose "complete knowledge of the real nature of the world, acting as a *quieter* of the will, produces resignation, the giving up not merely of life, but of the whole will-to-live itself." Schopenhauer also dismissed the "demand for so-called poetic justice" as "a dull, insipid, optimistic, Protestant-rationalistic, or really Jewish view of the world." Jim's death would be tragic, in Schopenhauer's view, not because it is just but because it is not; it exemplifies "the guilt of existence itself," on which Schopenhauer quotes the famous lines from Calderon's *La Vida es Sueño,* which Conrad also used, *"Pues el delito mayor / Del hombre es haber nacido"* ["For man's greatest offence / Is that he has been born"] (*World as Will and Representation.* Conrad used the couplet as the epigraph of *An Outcast of the Islands*).

A somewhat similar, but much more general, view of tragic conflict is that of Conrad's contemporary, Miguel de Unamuno, and it applies to the central theme of *Lord Jim* as a whole. The moral perspective of the three chief characters, Jim, Marlow, and Stein, is dominated by a sense of inexorable contradiction: for Jim it is his preoccupation with the intolerable discrepancy between what he has done and what he would like to have done; for Marlow it is the distance between his faith in solidarity and the apparently random and amoral meaninglessness of the physical and social world; for Stein it is the radical disjunction between the individual's ego-ideals and the world he struggles to realise them in. All three of these irremediable disjunctions exemplify what Unamuno called the tragic sense of life; and Jim's struggles can be seen as embodying Unamuno's affirmation that, despite his awareness of foredoomed defeat, the individual should nevertheless, like Don Quixote, live as though his faith were more real than any of the negations by which reason and experience alike demonstrate its futility.

Marlow exhibits a different, and later, phase of the same conflict. The pathos of Jim's presence sends Marlow's memory back to the defeated aspirations of his own youth; and this continual reminder is complemented by Marlow's increasingly bitter awareness that the code of solidarity is usually supported on grounds that are complacent or prudential, if they are not actually hypocritical; solidarity may be only the code of those whom experience has brought into an unprotesting conformity with the attitudes of their group. "The wisdom of life," Marlow remarks ironically, "consists in putting out of sight all the reminders of our folly, of our weakness, of our mortality." But Patusan exposes the triviality of such wisdom; there, Marlow discovers, "the haggard utilitarian lies of our civilisation wither and die," and in their place is revealed to Marlow a world "that seemed to wear a vast and dismal aspect of disorder." Of course, a more sheltered vision, Marlow sardonically reassures his comfortably established hearers, presents "in truth, thanks to our unwearied efforts . . . as sunny an arrangement of small conveniences as the mind of man can conceive."

His desolate irony at modern Western civilisation as a system of "small conveniences," is an indication not only of Marlow's tragic sense of life in general, but of how his way of seeing Jim has been transformed. The nature of this change is suggested in Marlow's letter to his privileged friend. The friend had argued that "we must fight in the ranks or our lives don't count," and that Jim's "kind of thing" in Patusan could only be "endurable and enduring when based on a firm conviction in the truth of ideas racially our own, in whose name are established the order, the morality of an ethical progress." Marlow replies that on this general position he can "affirm nothing," but that Jim's death forces him to wonder whether Jim, who "of all mankind . . . had no dealings but with himself . . . at the last . . . had not confessed to a faith mightier than the laws of order and progress."

Marlow does not name Jim's faith, but the immediate context

makes it clear that it belongs to a different and older phase of civilisation than that of modern "order and progress." The only such faith that has been mentioned in connection with Jim is Stein's diagnosis of him as romantic; but Marlow has earlier tended to equate "romantic" with an unrealistic, irresponsible and self-indulgent placing of the individual self above social norms. This equation, however, hardly does justice to Jim on Patusan, as Marlow realises. When Jim repeats his promise, "I shall be faithful," at their last parting, Marlow recalls Stein's romantic injunction "To follow the dream, and again to follow the dream—and so—always—*usque ad finem;*" and this leads Marlow to conclude of Jim that "He was romantic, but none the less true."

If we seek to find an ancient ideal of individual behaviour which can be called romantic, but which emphasises the obligation of being "true" and "faithful," it is surely to be found in medieval romance, which established both the word romantic and, long before, Europe's most distinctive and enduring ideal of personal conduct. That ideal has already been named, and given a kind of transcendental status, by the French Lieutenant: "The honour . . . that is real—that is!"

Honour is primarily associated, both in the chivalric romances and in common parlance, with the fame earned by exceptional exploits. Here Jim, who has filled Patusan "with the fame of his virtues," obviously qualifies. Serious doubts about his courage were raised by the *Patna* episode; but Jim's going to face Doramin constitutes the most dramatic refutation of the charge that on the *Patna* he had put his life above his honour; and it is surely this which makes Marlow believe that Jim's final act may have been "that supreme opportunity, that last and satisfying test for which I had always suspected him to be waiting." Jim may once have jumped, but when the last test comes he doesn't run away.

Jim's final act also gives him a supreme opportunity to embody two of the other key values of knightly honour: friendship and keeping faith. Jim's death is, in its way, an act of friendship for Dain Waris. Roland must not survive his comrade-in-arms Oliver. In obeying his pledge to Doramin, Jim is also implicitly keeping faith with Stein, Doramin's sworn comrade. Of course, to keep faith with Dain Waris, Doramin, and Stein, must entail betraying Jewel. Hers is the "jealous love" which Marlow must have in mind when he gives his final verdict on Jim: "We can see him, an obscure conqueror of fame, tearing himself out of the arms of a jealous love at the sign, at the call of his exalted egoism." The "sign" and the "call" refer back to Jewel's question about the nature of the mysterious power that would rob her of Jim: "Will it be a sign—a call?," she had asked Marlow. But after Jim's death, when Jewel asserts that Jim "was false," Stein protests. "Not false! True! true! true!"

The contradiction reflects how, although the code of honour, like that of solidarity, is based on approved social values, its more peremptory claims on the individual tend to convert it into a personal absolute, and thereby exalt it above all other obligations, whether public or private. It is their attitude to the claims of honour which makes Jewel and Stein see Jim's final choice differently. The depth of Jim's feeling for Jewel is not an issue: he "love[s] her dearly," and finds being "absolutely necessary" to her "wonderful"; the determining force, as Stein well understands, is the absolute nature of Jim's pledge. Jim obviously has this in mind when he says to Jewel that, if he were to respond to her appeal and flee Patusan, "I should not be worth having." The argument is a commonplace in the literature of honour; as Richard Lovelace put it in "To Lucasta, Going to the Wars": "I could not love thee (Dear) so much / Loved I not honour more."

When Marlow refers to Jim's faith as "exalted egoism," he is in effect repeating the common Stoic and Christian objection to the code of honour, an objection repeated in such later political and ethical philosophies as those of Montesquieu, Rousseau, and Kant. The basis of their objections is essentially that suggested by Marlow's statement that Jim "had no dealings but with himself": honour encourages a personal pride and self-sufficiency which leads the individual to put his primary trust in himself, instead of relying on divine grace, moral virtue, civic duty, or personal feeling.

That such charges can fairly be made against Jim, and against the code of honour in general, is incontestable; on the other hand, the gravity of the charges is not indisputable. It can be argued that contradictions arise when any theoretical system of behaviour is brought to the test of practice, and that, in "trying to save from the fire his idea of what his moral identity should be," Jim is trying to save an identity which has clearly incorporated a loyalty to the Western ethical tradition. This is made clear in Jim's dealings with Brown. For instance, when Brown says "even a trapped rat can give a bite," Jim immediately answers, "Not if you don't go near the trap till the rat is dead." It is clear that he knows very well what the safest course would be, but Jim would betray himself if he acted accordingly; the code of chivalric honour requires that an enemy should be treated with charity and as a human equal. So Jim asks "Will you promise to leave the coast?" When Brown agrees, and then breaks his word, it is not Jim who is dishonoured, as he would have been had he gone against his conscience.

His fatal generosity towards Brown is the climactic example of how, on Patusan, both Jim's romantic idealism and his rigid sense of personal honour have been shown to have a strong social and ethical component; and it is this component, rather than the "egoism and pride" of which Guerard speaks, which is primarily responsible for the catastrophe. Jim's personal allegiance to the heroic ideal is only involved to the extent that, when all else is lost he prefers to die rather than to live on with the sense that he has broken his troth and thus—and this time consciously—betrayed his conception of himself.

When Marlow speaks of Jim's "pitiless wedding with a shadowy ideal of conduct," the words "pitiless" and "shadowy" suggest that he has considerable reservations about the code of honour. In this Marlow reflects the whole modern intellectual and psychological outlook, which tends to see the code of honour as rigid, inhumane and retrograde; it suggests the stuffy and hypocritical moralism of the Victorian public school, as we are incidentally reminded in Jim's only use of the word—the old schoolboy oath of fidelity, "Honour bright." Many features of Jim's character no doubt exemplify Hannah Arendt's view that the psychological effect of the British colonial system tended to "a certain conservation, or perhaps petrification, of boyhood noblesse which preserved *and* infantilized Western moral standards" (*Origins of Totalitarianism*). Conrad, however, would probably have regarded a degree of intellectual callowness as a price well worth paying in exchange for fixed principles of honour; and all the evidence suggests that he saw Jim's character in this perspective. In his preface to *The Red Badge of Courage,* for instance, Conrad discussed its hero in a way which applies quite closely to Jim's shame after the *Patna*. Crane's Young Soldier, Conrad writes, is "the symbol of all untried men"; his fear does not make "him a morbid case" because "the lot of the mass of mankind is to know fear"; and Conrad then specifies that he means "the decent fear of disgrace." The fear of disgrace, in a somewhat different form, is also defended in the Author's Note to *Lord Jim*. There Conrad mentions that a lady had once objected to the novel as "morbid," and to this he retorts huffily that "no Latin temperament would have perceived anything morbid in the acute consciousness of lost honour." The ideal of honour, as Conrad here implies, tends to be Latin, Catholic and communal, rather than Germanic, Protestant and individual; it is also distinctively masculine, noble and secular; all these are values to which Conrad had been predisposed by his national and family traditions. It can, indeed, be argued that Conrad's emphasis on solidarity essentially derives from a chivalric tradition of honour which had continued to animate the Polish nobility long after it had been replaced or transformed elsewhere.

Lord Jim, indeed, reflects this by presenting a continuous confrontation between the exalted ideal of personal honour on the one hand, and the more modern, more widely applicable, but much more prosaic collective values of the code of solidarity on the other. In that conflict Conrad found himself siding more and more with his ancestral inheritance, and its ideal of individual honour; though possibly fated to isolation and failure in the modern world, it nevertheless possessed an unmediated directness of personal application, and a nostalgic heroic resonance, which Marlow's conception of solidarity was found to lack.

Lord Jim was André Gide's favourite among Conrad's novels, and it was its "despairing nobility" that he singled out for admiration. This gives a particular significance to a letter in which Gide told Conrad that if he were ever to write an article about him it would be to Alfred de Vigny and "to him alone, that I would wish to establish your kinship." Like Conrad, Alfred de Vigny was a nobleman, a stoic, and a disillusioned romantic; both men combined deeply isolated natures with an emphasis on a collective ethic which had its roots in their careers of professional service—although in Vigny's case as an officer of the infantry rather than of the merchant navy. In the peroration of his Souvenirs de servitude et grandeur militaire (1835), Vigny wrote that honour was the only lamp still left "which keeps its vigil in us like the last lamp in a devastated temple." The devastation was that caused by modern unbelief; but being a "purely human virtue that seems born from the earth," honour had outlasted all other creeds.

In some form, honour, and its corresponding human and artistic style, nobility, are timeless and indispensable values; and they continue to find exemplars or admirers even in the most relativist and sceptical climates of thought. Wallace Stevens once observed that "there is no element more conspicuously absent from contemporary poetry than nobility ("The Noble Rider and the Sound of Words"). If the statement were extended to modern fiction, Conrad, and especially *Lord Jim,* would be conspicuous exceptions. Jim does something which no other hero of a great twentieth-century novel has done: he dies for his honour. His action embodies Stein's dispiriting truth that "one thing alone can us from being ourselves cure!"; still, in his style of being cured, Jim implicitly confirms Stein's view that although, unlike the creatures of nature, man is not a masterpiece, by refusing to settle for less he can be amazing.

Narrative and Authority in *Lord Jim*: Conrad's Art of Failure

Suresh Raval

> *And that's the end. He passes away under a cloud, inscrutable at heart, forgotten, unforgiven, and excessively romantic. Not in the wildest days of his boyish visions could he have seen the alluring shape of such an extraordinary success! . . . we can see him an obscure conqueror of fame, tearing himself out of the arms of a jealous love at the sign, at the call of his exalted egoism. He goes away to celebrate his pitiless wedding with a shadowy ideal of conduct. Is he satisfied—quite, now, I wonder? We ought to know. He is one of us—and have I not stood up once, like an evoked ghost, to answer for his eternal constancy? Was I so very wrong after all? Now he is no more, there are days when the reality of his existence comes to me with an immense, with an overwhelming force; and yet upon my honor there are moments, too, when he passes from my eyes like a disembodied spirit astray among the passions of this earth, ready to surrender faithfully to the claim of his own world of shades.*
>
> *Who knows? He is gone, inscrutable at heart, and the poor girl is leading a sort of soundless, inert life in Stein's house. Stein has aged greatly of late. He feels it himself, and says often that he is "preparing to leave all this; preparing to leave. . . ." while he waves his hand sadly at his butterflies.*
>
> —Marlow, *Lord Jim*

These are Marlow's concluding words of the story of Jim's life, of his own response to Jim; they also end *Lord Jim*. But they do not signal for Marlow a conclusive response to Jim, nor do they signal for the reader the possibility of a reading that would decipher both the meaning of Jim's life and the meaning of *Lord Jim* in an unambiguous

From *ELH* 48, no. 2 (Summer 1981). © 1981 by the Johns Hopkins University Press, Baltimore/London.

mode. The ending is a compound of poignancy, confidence, and uncertainty, perhaps best characterized as profoundly disturbed and disturbing ambivalence, an ambivalence that seems to show the inadequacy of language, yet one that we cannot know or feel as ambivalence without language. The statement "We ought to know" deepens into the rhetorical question "Was I so very wrong after all," a response that seemingly implies a positive answer. Yet, by referring us back to his narrative of Jim, it implies further questions about Marlow's response to Jim. The ambiguity of the end of *Lord Jim* culminates in Marlow's final question, a question that puts Marlow's own interpretation of Jim into question and, more significantly, invites the reader to engage in the process of interpreting Jim again. Marlow thus speaks in a double epistemological mode: one emphasizes the inscrutable nature of Jim, whereas the other insists on Jim as "one of us." His narrative is therefore inconclusive, since he admits that he cannot declare the truth about Jim, that Jim remains an enigma to him, that his being "one of us" remains in a peculiar way indistinguishable from his compelling but enigmatic power over us.

What, then, is the nature of authority that Marlow can claim for his narrative? What is the nature of Marlow's knowledge of Jim, and what does his memorial reconstruction of Jim seek to achieve? These questions are crucial to an understanding of *Lord Jim* because they are implicit in Marlow's narrative as well as in the structure of the novel. For almost from the beginning Marlow suggests that he cannot claim real knowledge of Jim: "I wanted to know—and to this day I don't know, I can only guess." Marlow thus speaks, not from a vantage point of knowledge and certainty, but with an awareness that understanding does not possess a spontaneous clarity in the mind, which he can with difficulty articulate in words. Language itself, moreover, poses further problems, since, as he says, "the power of sentences has nothing to do with their sense or the logic of their construction." Consequently, Marlow's narrative proceeds in a self-questioning mode: "I don't pretend I understood him. The views he let me have of himself were like those glimpses through the shifting rents in a thick fog—bits of vivid and vanishing detail, giving no connected idea of the general aspect of a country. . . . Upon the whole he was misleading."

Marlow's narrative, then, is an expression of a knot of complications: language is problematical; his own understanding of Jim is not clear; and Jim himself is misleading. No doubt each one of these features is sufficient for complicating Marlow's as well as our own response to Jim; yet in *Lord Jim* all three features are meshed together in such a manner that for Marlow the success of his narrative is closely interwoven with his admission of its failure to clearly grasp Jim. It is not as if Marlow's self-deprecatory remarks, or his uncertainty, or his narrative duplicity is merely the product of a gentle irony, an irony that has matured through a prior, shattering experience of Kurtz in *Heart of Darkness*. For just as Kurtz's experience "is posited outside Marlow's discourse" [as Edward W. Said points out], so too is Jim's experience exterior to Marlow's narrative, though by claiming Jim as "one of us" Marlow seeks to appropriate that experience. Marlow is therefore aware that in a strict sense his authority is a sham, but he remains committed to his project of bringing Jim within the empirical bounds of human understanding, even at the cost of duplicity. For example, Marlow sees that if the unexpected erupted in Jim's life, it could occur in anyone else's life, as it did in Razumov's in *Under Western Eyes*. Real failure would consist in the possibility that, given the inscrutable nature of Jim's experience, no attempt is made to record and articulate it for us. It is therefore inevitable that Marlow should perceive Brierly's suicide as a refusal to confront and grasp the implications for human existence of Jim's fatal jump from the *Patna*.

Marlow's perception of the duplicity and inauthenticity of human life as it is ordinarily lived constitutes a central urge behind his interest in Jim. He recognizes in Jim's facing of the trial "a redeeming feature in his abominable case." In an important sense, then, Marlow has, despite the pervasive ambiguity in his narrative, made a judgment of Jim, and the judgment is a positive one. It consists in his feeling, reinforced by Brierly's suicide, that Jim's is an exemplary case: "I hadn't been so sure of it before." It is, however, not a question of mere confirmation of this certainty, but a question of not being able to ground this certainty in any finality of response which constitutes the center of Marlow's narrative. For Marlow cannot sum up Jim's life, or his response to it, in some irreducible and essential meaning: "End! Finis! the potent word that exorcises from the house of life the haunting shadow of fate. This is what—notwithstanding the testimony of my eyes and his own earnest assurances—I miss when I look back upon Jim's success. . . . He was not—if I may say so—clear to me. He was not clear. And there is a suspicion he was not clear to himself either." Clarity, self-understanding—the goals of an epistemology of the self—are thus put beyond the possibility of attainment, though, paradoxically, these goals are among the motivating factors that put in motion Marlow's narrative and the reader's interest.

There is thus a contradiction at the heart of Marlow's narrative, though it is not a straightforward logical contradiction. Rather it operates in the form of sliding so that if at one point Marlow seems to assert one thing, soon he asserts another. This sliding suggests a shifting of the ground of his interest in Jim. It can be construed as involving a logical contradiction if we translate Marlow's responses at different junctures into specific propositions. Take, for instance, Marlow's explanation of his initial interest in Jim: "I wanted to see him overwhelmed, confounded, pierced through and through, squirming like an impaled beetle." This is a moral response stemming from his feeling that Jim "stood there for all the parentage of his kind . . . whose very existence is based upon honest faith, and upon the instinct of courage." If Jim is thus a representative of humanity, Marlow needs no other grounds for his interest in Jim. Yet Marlow has another, more compelling ground for that interest: "I have a distinct notion I wished to find something. Perhaps unconsciously, I hoped I would find that something, some merciful explanation, some convincing shadow of an excuse. I see well now that I hoped for the impossible—for the laying of what is the most obstinate ghost of man's creation . . . the doubt of the sovereign power enthroned in a fixed standard of conduct." If Marlow's first response was to see Jim experience moral agony, the second shares with it its moral drive in a contradictory fashion. It shows that along with a desire to see Jim morally "squirming" there existed in Marlow the desire to find some excuse for Jim. At another level, however, from the perspective of Marlow's many encounters with Jim that he describes until the end of chapter 35, Marlow recognizes that his interest in Jim stemmed from a prior skeptical feeling that the code of conduct had no absolute authority over human life.

Marlow's desire to seek an explanation, and to provide a justification, for Jim's history is necessarily a drive to seek objective content, to discover objective significance, and to communicate it to his listeners. Its foremost task is that of comprehending a human being whose transgression does not minimize his human significance. That is why Marlow insists, "You must understand he did not try to minimize its importance . . . therein lies his distinction."

Marlow, however, doubts his narrative ability because he doubts his capacity for seeing innocently or with the epistemological certainty which is presumed to make him a representative of his profession. Consequently, his narrative, though about Jim, also turns into one about himself, about his own potential transgressions, about the impossibility of pure allegiance to one's values, the impossibility of fulfilling the dream which Jim himself never abandons.

As I will try to show in this essay, Marlow's narrative is more profound than his explicit interpretive remarks suggest, for these remarks also indicate his moments of failure to understand. His narrative therefore contains implicitly and through distortions interpretive sign-posts which disclose Marlow's failure and exceed his intention partly by contradicting it. Yet this contradiction cannot sustain itself without showing at the same time in Marlow's interpretation a quality of response that will signal his listeners' willingness to entertain Marlow's apprehension of Jim. The reader consequently is implicated in a movement of contradiction and is at the same time forced to carry on an activity of decipherment that Marlow must, caught in his own contradiction, leave unarticulated. Moreover, the transgressor, Jim, seeks a mode of being that, in his effort to realize it, not only brings to light the fundamental inadequacies of all modes of (human) being, but also succeeds in a way that is not separable from failure. The narrative of *Lord Jim* therefore pulls and strains in ways that reveal contradictions as conjunctions, success as failure, and ideals as perversion. It discloses the necessity of ideals for the effective functioning of the community, but it at the same time discloses the ideals as possessing an inhuman and absolute status in human life. If they seem human and necessary for life in one context, they seem inhuman and destructive in another context. Each context implicitly leads to the other, and neither is unquestionable.

II

Marlow's encounters with the French lieutenant, the German merchant and entomologist, and Jewel are among the most important moments in his narrative, moments when he seeks to invest his narrative with authority. Each provides Marlow with a different vantage point on Jim, and each complicates his understanding of Jim. The immediate perspective that each offers on Jim at once opens up the gulf between them on the one hand and Jim on the other. For instance, the French lieutenant has stood the test of experience, whereas Jim has failed it; Stein has proved himself in the past by combining practical action with romantic idealism, whereas Jim, driven by the same longing, has not; Jewel has initially made an unromantic acceptance of failure as the basis of her life, whereas Jim, defiantly self-assertive, has in a sense lured her into the circle of his illusion.

The French lieutenant represents the authority of practical reason and experience, an authority that derives its power, not from an unqualified assertion of the self, but from a recognition of the self's liabilities. For instance, he says: "Each of them . . . if he were an honest man . . . would confess . . . that there is somewhere a point when you let go everything . . . Given a certain combination of circumstances, fear is sure to come." He thus does not present himself in the light of an exalted ideal of self. Instead, he admits: "Man is born a coward . . . It is a difficulty—*parbleu!* It would be too easy otherwise. But habit—habit—necessity—do you see?—the eye of others—*voila*. One puts up with it. And then the example of others who are no better than yourself, and yet make good countenance." This is the clearest, because the most unpretentious, statement of the code of conduct. It defines and delimits the question of personal authority; and it perceives a relation between fear and courage. The strength of the lieutenant's perception resides in his refusal to allow this relation to undermine the authority of the code of conduct. For he says: "one may get on knowing very well that one's courage does not come of itself (*ne vient pas tout seul*). There is nothing much in that to get upset about. One truth the more ought not to make life impossible . . . the honour . . . The honour . . . that is real—that is! And what life may be worth when . . . the honour is gone . . . I can offer no opinion—because . . . I know nothing of it." The French lieutenant here recognizes the possibility of failure of courage, or rather the possibility of overcoming of oneself by fear; but he does not allow it to open any skeptical reflection on life.

Courage, as the French lieutenant says, is grounded in habit, a practice learned in the community of other men. It is not the result of either conscious reflection or deliberate preparedness, but is manifested in obedient and decisive action. It does not imply elimination of the instinct of fear; rather it implies a restraint on fear by the practical exercises of daily living. Courage, in other words, is the result of an action grounded in the moral dictates of the community;

it brings one honor, and contributes to the stability and health of the community. Nevertheless, the code, as held by the members of a community, tends to possess a transcendental ontological status. For as the French lieutenant explains, honor depends on the fulfillment of the code of one's craft, and this honor is real since it grants moral sanction to one's life. Consequently, for the lieutenant, despite his recognition of the overwhelming nature of the instinct of fear, the code, ostensibly a matter of habitual obedience, is inflexible. If honor is gone, one's life could have no meaning or justification.

Though sprung from the pragmatic context of human transactions, the code thus demands an unswerving allegiance and possesses a status not justified by either the instinct or the possibility of experience. To the extent, then, that the French lieutenant acknowledges the power of fear and the possibility of failure, his watch on the *Patna* for thirty hours can claim to be not an exemplary act but simply a performance of duty. The helmsman at the inquiry, we remember, gives a list of names that puts the French lieutenant's action in a long-standing tradition of seamanship. The lieutenant admits that he wouldn't know what to do or say when honor is gone, an admission that recognizes one's helplessness before failure. It is, moreover, an admission that refuses to engage in reflective thought about transgression and its implications for human action and intention. From the pragmatic perspective, however, that is as it should be. Yet the refusal to ponder further discloses the code's inhuman, transcendental status, for it concedes the authority of the court to conduct its inquiry on the assumption that a transgression of the code under any circumstances is an unmitigable offense.

Contrary to the view of some critics, then, the French lieutenant's conduct does not necessarily undermine Jim's. Similarly, the elitist perspective that finds the lieutenant repudiated by Marlow's privileging of the importance of the quality of one's feeling or consciousness is not correct either. Both perspectives are, of course, allowed a play, but neither is dominant. They co-exist with others in a movement that constitutes the ambiguity of *Lord Jim,* not reducible to the certitudes of any perspective. For if the quality of feeling alone mattered, it would do so only by a denial of the pragmatic context of simple virtues disclosed in the fulfillment of daily obligations. Brierly's suicide, to take a concrete example, does not simply confirm the impossibility of an unqualified assertion of the self. By a contradictory movement it also confirms the necessity and importance of the French lieutenant's action. If, to take another example, the helmsman and the French lieutenant seem heroically to mock Jim, Jim seems to mock them by a heroic gesture of self-assertion. Neither response by itself is adequate, and each requires the other to comprehend *Lord Jim*. The oscillation of response that occurs in the novel is extremely complex, and functions at the level of a fundamental questioning of the nature of authority and its relation to Marlow's narration of Jim's story.

If the French lieutenant is antithetical to Jim, the German merchant, Stein, is closer to Jim by an affinity for adventure which in itself had little value for the lieutenant. Stein possesses, in addition, a reflective bent, and presents a sharp contrast to the French lieutenant. Marlow comes to Stein for advice in the matter of Jim. And the advice is stated in what are perhaps Stein's most notoriously ambiguous remarks:

> A man that is born falls into a dream like a man who falls into the sea. If he tries to climb out into the air as inexperienced people endeavor to do, he drowns—*nicht wahr?* . . .
> The way is to the destructive element submit yourself, and with the exertions of your hands and feet in the water make the deep, deep sea keep you up.

On this account man cannot live without some ideals, but ideals tend to possess a destructive power. Yet those who seek to live without them cannot find happiness. For instance, the fat captain disappears; Chester is destroyed by a tornado; Gentleman Brown, consumed by hatred and disease, dies; Brierly, with a misplaced moral passion but acknowledging the hollowness of his ideal, commits suicide; and Stein withdraws into a mode of living that has no connection with the heroic nature of the struggle invoked by his metaphor of the dream. Moreover, Stein's dream, initially a life-sustaining vision, has emptied itself of its moral content and assumed the shape of passivity and meaninglessness exemplified in his collection of dead butterflies.

To return to the passage quoted above, Stein holds out for man an imperative of endurance because ideals are both necessary and destructive. The imperative amounts to this: make your ideals help you to live. But why, one may ask, such a tragic imperative from a romantic idealist? Stein's answer here is unequivocal: "Man is come where he is not wanted, where there is no room for him." Thus there is an antithetical relation between man and the natural world. Indeed, man has the burden of living in the hostile, natural world, and therefore creates ideals that make it possible for him to live. This situation is complicated by the fact that man is also driven by antithetical desires: "We want in so many different ways to be." This contradiction, or ambivalence, fundamental to human life, makes it impossible for man to live in harmony either with the natural world which is not his proper habitat since he cannot live without ideals, or with his ideal which is opposed to the world since it is the product of his imagination and desire. Man's ideals are the "destructive element" because he can neither live without them nor make them natural to the world in which he has to live. As a result man can never realize his ideal. Thus if the natural world is brutal, and man's ideals are destructive, Stein's advice would amount to this: forge a possibility of life out of that which is liable to enclose and destroy you.

Stein, however, cannot give this advice because he has already insisted on the inevitability of failure: "Because you not always can keep your eyes shut, there comes the real trouble—the heart pain—the world pain . . . it is not good for you to find you cannot make your dream come true, for the reason that you not strong enough are, or not clever enough." In other words, man's imagination and strength cannot subdue the natural world whose contingencies invade and destroy man's fondest hopes. Nor can they control and manipulate the ideal whose inexorable logic subverts man's best intentions. Stein's attempt to give Marlow advice cannot succeed because his imperative of endurance is radically at odds with his construal of man's contradictory spiritual make-up. It is therefore inevitable that Stein should not be able to answer his question: "So if you ask me—how to be." "His twitching lips uttered no word, and the austere exaltation of a certitude seen in the dusk vanished from his face."

That is, of course, Marlow's interpretation of Stein's response to the question "how to be." Marlow's own response to Stein and Jim not only suggests a gulf between Stein and Jim but also indicts Stein for the problematical and questionable nature of his own survival in the "destructive element." For long before Jim's ideal will reveal its destructive nature, Stein has been living its ghostlier version whose chief features are mere survival and reflection on his butterflies. The logic of Stein's contradictory response, then, resides in the "heart pain," the "world pain," for though he would like to advocate the imperative of endurance, Stein still wants to realize his ideal through the surrogate self he sees in Jim. Stein consequently denies his own imperative in sending Jim to Patusan, a remote island province which is the place of his former triumph and eventual failure. Through Jim Stein seeks to reconstitute the self that failed the test of experience. Stein's words, far from constituting an advice for Jim, represent his own antithetical drives, though these drives are no longer connected to direct participation in action. Stein's authority thus reveals itself, at the moment of its assertion, to be inauthentic.

From Stein and the French lieutenant Marlow sought advice, some moral grounds for excusing Jim's lapse, just as Jim himself seeks from Marlow a means of "absolution." From his encounter with Jewel, however, Marlow does not seek advice or help for Jim. For if the French lieutenant has sympathized with Jim, and if Stein has seen his own younger romantic self in Jim, they both at least believe in his transgression committed in the grip of fear. Jewel, on the contrary, refuses to believe that. Yet she has an unfailing intuition that he is haunted by some private demon and will one day leave her to follow it. Consequently, she, too, like Jim, seeks some sort of release from a painful knowledge of the past. Unlike Jim, however, she is not responsible for it. It is this difference that guides her at first in wishing that Jim leave Patusan before she feels his love for her and therefore knows happiness in life. Prior to Jim's arrival in Patusan, and some time after, she has been viciously abused by Cornelius, Stein's agent who married her mother when Jewel's father abandoned both mother and child. She had no other knowledge of the world from where Jim has come to Patusan; "all that she knew of its inhabitants were a betrayed woman [her mother] and a sinister pantaloon [Cornelius]." Inevitably, Marlow's encounter with Jewel leaves him feeling that her life is unalterably tragic, that she is the very "spectre of fear."

Almost from the beginning Marlow realizes that love has not brought Jewel happiness, "as if fear and incertitude had been the safeguards of her love." On her insistent questioning why Jim would not return to his society, Marlow replies, "Because he is not good enough." Jewel, of course, rejects the answer as a lie. To take the sting out of his remark Marlow tells her, "Nobody, nobody is good enough." For Jewel, however, Jim's character is unquestionable. The conversation, then, does not bring any relief to Jewel. But it is shat-

tering to Marlow. He loses his normal sense of composure and experiences an "utter defeat" before Jewel's unconsolable questioning.
"The very ground on which I stood seemed to melt under my feet."
And he acutely experiences the impossibility of communication with
her: "It was impossible to make her understand. I chafed silently at
my impotence."

The skeptical consequence of Marlow's encounter with Jewel is
a remarkable moment in *Lord Jim*, because neither the French lieutenant nor Stein had shattered the authoritative consciousness that
characterizes Marlow's response to them. Marlow's description, for
instance, of the parting between himself and the French lieutenant
stands in sharp contrast to his sense of "utter defeat" with Jewel. If
the first occasion ends in a grotesque posturing of civilized amenity,
a comedy at the heart of ordinary life, the second ends with a
wrenching sense of failure, a tragic knowledge that Jewel's life is
wrought in tragedy and that she is as inaccessible as Jim. Marlow's
meeting with Stein also ended with a melancholy reflection, yet had
a positive aspect to it. Stein seemed to Marlow an older version of
Jim, and evoked a hope that Jim may yet master his fate on Patusan.
But with Jewel Marlow seemed to lose all conviction. Marlow's
characterization of Jim and Jewel is very apt: "They had mastered
their fates. They were tragic." Thus Jim has mastered his fate by
mastering its very source, fear, by becoming fearless, whereas Jewel
has mastered her fate by becoming the very "spectre of fear." Jim's
fearlessness and Jewel's fear together constitute a powerful contradiction, one that is rendered ironic by their conjunction. I want to
discuss, in the next section of this essay, the implications of such
contradictions and conjunctions for Marlow's narrative.

Lord Jim, as we have discussed so far, dramatizes the vectors of
the mind's relationship to its desires. The French lieutenant insists on
both the necessity of subservience of desire to duty and the mutual
implication of fear and courage. Brierly, on the other hand, cannot
accept the subservience of desire to duty, but rather sees them as
equivalent. For him the principle of authority invested in the self is
unquestionable. Consequently, when Jim's case compels him to see
the untruth in his concept, life becomes unacceptable to him. Stein
had once tried to live a life that would combine practical action with
idealism. Yet, despite his initial success, he admits to Marlow that
many times he had let the dream pass. His confident moralizing tone,
intent on explaining "how to be," thus changes into an admission of

failure. He cannot provide a principle of authority. Neither can Jewel. Indeed, she brings Marlow to the very brink of epistemological uncertainty. And it is from the vantage point of this uncertainty that Marlow's narrative seeks to interpret Jim.

Since there is no true or absolute authority, Marlow must from time to time put his narrative into question, and claim for it only contingent authority, for even the act of putting into question is an act claiming some sort of authority. Without such a claim, Marlow could not characterize Jim as an enigma. Jim would, then, be left as an object of contempt or embarrassment as with Brierly, good only for exploitation as with the Australian desperado, Chester. Marlow's perspective thus differs from the perspectives of both the French lieutenant and Stein, though it cannot traverse the distance between itself and Jim's own experience. This distance, interpreted, reflected, puzzled over, and at times repudiated by Marlow, constitutes the nub of the enigmatic nature of Lord Jim, of Jim himself, and of Marlow's narrative. The structure of the novel is conceived on a foundation that is itself hollow. For it is a labyrinthine structure with perspectives within perspectives which do not converge upon any unquestionable single understanding but rather disclose an absence of true knowing. Jim remains an other, a tantalizing figure of the imagination that is not finally known, but only caught in a web of words that remain sincere yet duplicitous, disturbingly true in their impact, yet contingent and inauthentic, proximate to our knowledge of ourselves and our uncertainty about that knowledge yet distant by virtue of their disclosure that Jim is a fictional character. The compelling power of Jim as a fictional character therefore resides in the complicated mediation between fact and fiction that he represents.

III

The narrative of Lord Jim constitutes a search for an explanation of the meaning of Jim, not simply as a solitary individual, but as an individual whose enigmatic solidarity with mankind Marlow unequivocally asserts. For Marlow this solidarity is defined by a capacity to feel: "The thing is that in virtue of his feeling he mattered." At the moment, then, of telling the story, Marlow's interest in Jim cannot be ascribed to an illusory hope that through Jim he may overcome "that doubt which is the inseparable part of our knowledge." If the code of conduct has no absolute basis, if its truth is not separable from its illusory nature, then what matters is the relation that obtains between one's consciousness and the code of conduct; the relation, in other words, that one's intentions have to one's actions and their ramifications in the private and public spheres of one's life. The narrative of *Lord Jim* seeks to capture this relation by explicating, deciphering, and translating the signs that make up the complex and elusive context of Jim's life.

Lord Jim thus comprises a system of signs; and the signs are necessarily plural, and exceed any stated intention of either Marlow or the impersonal narrator. Any deciphering of these signs must therefore require many criteria, and the criteria must themselves be established by two contradictory viewpoints. First, there is the inescapable fact of Jim's fatal jump from the *Patna*. On an obvious level, this weakness is not something finally overcome and transcended, but is rather repeated and renewed in another crucial failing which must remain forever concealed from him. Second, there is Jim's attempt to purchase his innocence, or to expiate his guilt, an attempt which completely entraps him within his desired conception of self. The logic of this contradiction requires that guilt and innocence must not remain opposites or contraries but rather coexist as mutually interdependent sources that make up the fractured modality of the human self.

Marlow's own narrative discloses a conception of his own self which participates in this consciousness of the fissure in the self. For example, Marlow says: "I at least had no illusions; but it was I, too, who a moment ago had been so sure of the power of words, and now was afraid to speak." His effort to understand Jim and to make him accessible to others is already beset with insuperable difficulties, first because he finds language inadequate to the task which he must undertake, and second because Marlow has an acute consciousness of having been left "strangely unenlightened" by his experience of Jim. Marlow's fragmented narrative, however, is not a deliberate mystification on his part, but the necessity lying at the heart of his response to Jim. For though Jim remains an enigma, he is, paradoxically, a form of revelation. Jim, for instance, surrounds and protects the ideal he has conceived of himself, and at the same time remains imprisoned within that very ideal.

Marlow's avowals therefore do not undermine his own response to Jim and turn his figuration of Jim into a mystification; instead, his avowals confirm that figuration in a disturbing manner. The enigmatic Jim is "one of us," he is a necessity lying in our own selves. For Jim constitutes for Marlow a profoundly complex reality of human aspirations, a reality upon which Marlow attempts to confer the stability and solidity of a perceived object. Hence the impressionistic technique in Marlow's narrative, a technique which has important consequences for the structure of *Lord Jim*. Consider, for instance, the task of language to present Jim as an enigma. The task is a highly complex one, since an enigma is by definition intractable to the representational powers of language. Nevertheless, because it is an enigma, it has to be presented in a language that discloses the inadequacy of language. Consequently, that which is intractable to language must be re-presented in language in order to repudiate the latter. Such a repudiation itself, however, must occur in language and thus empower language with self-reflexivity initially shown to be lacking in it. If, as Marlow puts it, "words . . . belong to the sheltering conception of light and order which is our refuge," Marlow's problem is to strain language against itself. The triumph of language, which is the same as the triumph of consciousness (since neither is conceivable without the other), is therefore announced at the very moment when its inadequacy is announced and confirmed.

Given the necessary ambiguity of his response to Jim, Marlow must attempt a technique of evasion and fragmentation, a technique of seemingly alternative views which are sometimes offered as opposed views but which sometimes turn out to be simplified versions of the ideal represented by Jim. The Conradian universe is thus fragmented. There is no Logos which can bring together and unite its fragmented stories into a totality; there is no Logos which comprehends them and refers them to the finality of a truth which makes for the meaning and possibility of confident moral action. For instance, Marlow, admitting the impossibility of saying the last words about Jim, says: "Are not our lives too short for that full utterance which through all our stammerings is of course our only and abiding intention." For the link between self and the world on the one hand and on the other the truths that are presumed to give a solidity and wholeness to self and the world is absent. Jim's steadfast holding to an egoistic moral conception of self thus conceals a more profound, fragmentary, and self-destructive human reality.

The entanglements of Marlow's narrative have therefore given up searching for a unity which would coalesce the different and conflicting parts, a unity which would totalize the fragments. The narrative, straining toward an aesthetic of idealism, causes ruptures in that aesthetic and introduces movements that put into question the nostalgia for a reconciliation of opposites. The principle of reconciliation sees art as a drama of opposite or contradictory forces emerging in formal harmony variously defined as tragedy, as comedy, or as tragi-comedy. The modernist strain in fiction, however, of which *Lord Jim* is a supreme exemplar, brings about fundamental generic distortions in our expectations from literary experience. Marlow's narrative is thus in search of a form that would comprehend his uncertainty caused and complicated by Jim's own response to his actions. As Marlow says, "What I could never make up my mind about was whether his line of conduct amounted to shirking his ghost or to facing him out . . . as with the complexion of all our actions, the shade of difference was so delicate that it was impossible to say. It might have been flight and it might have been a mode of combat." By characterizing Jim in terms of "the complexion of all our actions" Marlow refuses to define Jim as a mere idealist aberration. Jim, in other words, embodies the unconscious story of all human life brought to the level of awareness in Marlow's narrative.

Hidden from Jim's knowledge of himself and foreshadowed in Marlow's narrative is a self that we may identify as a form of desire, narcissistic desire, which self-destructively turns in upon itself. Marlow's puzzled, though critical fascination with Jim, as our own with him, is an attempt to look this desire in the face. Yet that is precisely what cannot be done. Marlow's narrative as a result is a series of repetitions intended to traverse the distance and difference that remain between Jim's self that is captured in Marlow's interpretation, itself helped and hindered by Jim's own interpretation of himself, and Jim's self that remains inaccessible and in the form of this desire.

It is important to keep in mind that Jim's concept of self is rooted in both his community from which he learned his ideals, and his reading of books of romantic adventure from which he learned to give fictional shapes to his ideals. In this respect he is, like Don Quixote, a novelistic character. Don Quixote, everyone would agree, reads the world in order to prove the books he has read. Jim, too, would like to read the world in order to prove his ideal of conduct. He would like adventure to offer itself to him in a moment he can predict and control. He therefore cannot conceive of adventure as the naive fictional form of the contingent or the accidental. He cannot see that the contingent is not subject to a supervening will; otherwise, it could not be conceived as contingent. For Jim, however, the contingent is synonymous with the expected. In thus not recognizing the power of the contingent to subvert human intentions Jim has assimilated it within the boundaries of the rational or the predictable. The assimilation is a dangerous one, for he has reduced the inhuman to the level of the human. It is of course the consequence of the mind's desire to make its dominion on every condition of life.

Yet the mind that desires the reduction of the inhuman to the human cannot realize that it is already itself contaminated by the inhuman. Jim's failure to realize this is illustrated in the second half of *Lord Jim* which is concerned with Jim's attempt to realize the dream in Patusan. His failure is given a trenchant ironic force by Jim's admission to Marlow of both his love for Jewel and his triumphant conviction that the people of Patusan trust him for their safety. Talking of his love for Jewel, Jim says, "You take a different view of your actions when you come to understand, when you are *made* to understand every day that your existence is necessary . . . to another person. I am made to feel that." And talking of the people of Patusan, Jim says, "I must go on, go on for ever holding up my end, to feel sure that nothing can touch me. I must stick to their belief in me to feel safe and to . . . keep in touch . . . with those whom, perhaps, I shall never see any more." Jim has thus put his relationship with both Jewel and the people of Patusan, love and public role, in a context which is defined for him by his transgression on the *Patna*. However, the larger context of his ideal by which he seeks to invest his self with authority already contains the seeds of its own destruction, and leads Jim once again on the path to failure.

Jim's entrapment within his ideal is so thorough that he continues to defend it even when it has become severed from the context in which it possessed its significance. This entrapment is at the basis of Jim's failure to understand Gentleman Brown. And it is at the basis of his failure in self-understanding. There is, of course, a compelling reason behind Jim's response: he refuses to make arbitrary judgments of good and bad. The inquiry into the *Patna* affair by the court has left Jim convinced that no amount of factual data could explain the psychological forces that made him jump. Moreover, to Jim his jump meant an act of unconscious identification with the other transgressors. Yet he saw himself as apart from them, separated by a morality of feeling that he has no grounds to attribute to his partners in the act. With Brown, however, Jim's response is more complex than that of unconscious identification. For though no direct incriminating evidence against Brown is available to him, his experience on the *Patna* has taught him to be wary of any such evidence. For example, after he has promised a clear road to Brown, Jim tells Jewel, "Men act badly sometimes without being much worse than others."

The tragic paradox of Jim's treatment of Brown, however, is that his failure on the *Patna* generates a moral insight that cannot provide him with discriminating powers to separate good from bad. Jim's predicament, then, resides in his being an exemplary moral agent whose insight does not just cause but rather reveals his moral blindness: it prevents him from using moral concepts. More precisely, Jim so thoroughly equates morality with his conception of the self that he cannot perceive that moral action is helped as well as hindered by others. Intentions, in other words, even if they are motivated by moral impulse, do not necessarily lead to commensurate moral consequences. Gentleman Brown, for instance, takes his frustrated revenge on Jim by killing Dain Waris and his party. Jim, on the contrary, seeks to redeem his honor by letting Dain's father, Doramin, take his life. The result of Jim's conflation of the code of conduct with his egoistic ideal of self is that he cannot understand the propriety of his act of martyrdom with regard either to Jewel or to the people of Patusan. Instead of giving him moral stability the ideal has now lost its intersubjective value and become detached and inhuman. It is put in the service of death rather than life. Jim's statement to Marlow that his life was necessary to Jewel, or that the people of Patusan trusted their safety to him, reveals a contradictory relation to his final moral posture. Jewel loses her love, and Patusan is once again open to desperadoes like Brown.

By a peculiar and inexorable logic of thought, however, Jim's final action is unavoidable. When, for instance, Jewel urges Jim to defend himself against Doramin because he had promised her that he would never leave her, Jim says, "I should not be worth having." From the vantage point of his ideal of self Jim's response is unanswerable. Nevertheless, the moral predicament of Jim's ideal is that it must remain detached from its consequences. Though sprung from the moral practices of his community it has lost its vital relation to those practices. Patusan is merely a dream-world where the ideal has its full sway for Jim. Enclosed in this solipsistic understanding of his

ideal, Jim cannot see that martyrdom and courage have little significance since they are no longer distinguishable from suicide. The
meanings of words—trust, honor, courage, and love—central to Jim's
action have lost their contextual stability or usefulness because the
contexts have become merged, because ideal and perversion have
become one. The tragic paradox of this sequence of events is that
where Jim had found his own self reflected in Gentleman Brown,
Doramin now finds Brown in Jim. The result of this inversion for
Jim is that while Jim says "Nothing can touch me," he is also cut
down by the most ruthless principle of revenge. At one level of
response a preparedness to accept punishment for his mistake certainly frees Jim from any potential ignominy others may seek to
attach to his character. Yet the narrative calls into play that response
only in order to complicate and contradict it. For the other, and more
compelling, response is that he has purchased his ideal at a spiritual
price that involves nothing less than a dehumanization of that self.

Jim, in a sense, does not have a choice because in order for him
to think of choice he will have to see himself confronting alternatives. The context of moral choice, in other words, involves a sense
of the strength of each available alternative, a sense that helps one
determine one's choice. Moreover, to experience the tension of alternatives is to make a judgment as to the importance and validity of
one's choice. Entrapped within his ideal, however, Jim cannot make
a choice; he is chosen by the ideal he has lived for; the ideal has
become his surrogate for living. He therefore cannot even think of
his situation in terms of alternatives. To Jewel's plea to fight or
escape, Jim replies: "There is nothing to fight for . . . nothing is
lost. . . . There is no escape." Jim has thus made a radical choice.
And it is inevitable that he should not think of his choice as the result
of a reflection on his moral predicament. Jim's radical choice does not
allow him to experience his situation as a moral dilemma, nor does
it allow him reflection on its consequences. For the Sartrean man
radical choice springs from a dilemma but also entails no looking
back or remorse on the part of the moral agent. Conrad's treatment
of Jim's radical choice, it seems to me, opens up a serious questioning
of the very concept of radical choice. Radical choice, from the perspective of *Lord Jim*, is always already infected by the element of
chance or contingency. The moral agent (in this case Jim) can escape
it only by a romantic idealization of self. The escape, however, is no
more than a failure of the consciousness to look upon one's capacity

for causing ruin in a moment and through a conjunction of forces over neither of which it has control. Marlow's description of Jim's state of mind clearly illustrates this point. After the news of Dain Waris's death, Jim tries to write a letter—to his father, to Marlow, or to those with whom he is trying to regain his solidarity. But he couldn't write. "The pen had spluttered, and that time he gave it up. There's nothing more; he had seen a broad gulf that neither eye nor voice could span. . . . He was overwhelmed by the inexplicable; he was overwhelmed by his own personality—the gift of that destiny which he had done his best to master." Thus the ideal that enabled Jim to invest his life with a semblance of order and hope has now brought him to a point when his choice reveals its radical incoherence.

Thus contrary to the French lieutenant who recognized that there is a gulf between fear and courage bridged only by an unromantic exercise of duty, Jim takes a radical step. He does not so much connect the two as squelches fear. He becomes fearless. Yet the code, we remember, is the result of a recognition of the instinct of fear, a recognition that requires courage for the functioning of the community. Jim's fearlessness, then, is a distortion of the human self, since the community perceives the self as a compound of fear and courage. Jim has therefore assumed an identity which has no connection with the community within which the code of conduct has its meaning and value. It is inevitable that Jim should not only allow himself to be shot by Doramin but also ignore Jewel's desperate but all-too-human plea to defend himself. For when courage separates itself from the context of other human instincts and relations, it has no place for love or responsibility. And it does not recognize the obstacles generated in one's conception of one's public identity by the fact of personal relations.

Nevertheless, to recognize Jim's last action as a revelation of the failure of his ideal and as a repetition of his jump from the *Patna* is to simplify both Marlow's response to Jim and the structure of *Lord Jim*. Indeed, Marlow, in telling the story of Jim's life and in seeking an articulation of his own responses to it, ventures on a forbidden territory for the context of practical life, for a reflection on Jim reveals a fundamental contradiction between the community's concept of moral life and the hidden possibilities within the self, a contradiction that Jim seeks to overcome through his refusal to conceive of human life as a compound of fear and courage. Jim cannot accept the self in its mundane role as entailing small victories and defeats incurred in the performance of one's duty. Yet it is not as if the community views its ideals as pragmatic, having no transcendental ontological status, for if it did, the door to radical skepticism would be opened. The French lieutenant, for instance, refuses to ponder the consequences of a possible loss of honor because he cannot conceive them apart from a denial of life itself. The community therefore cannot do without ascribing an absolute status to its ideals. Such a status, however, introduces a fundamental duplicity in the life of the community, since it pretends to bring skepticism under control, though at a deeper level it recognizes lying as a necessity in order that intersubjective action and responsibility become meaningful in human life.

This contradiction in the community's conception of its ideals is enabling rather than destructive, since its predication of life on the fulfillment of ideals is compatible with the possibility of failure. For Jim, however, fulfillment of the ideal fully depends on a denial of failure. Consequently, its fulfillment becomes synonymous with death. Yet if Jim is the product of the contradiction inherent in the community's life between practice and ideal, he is its exemplary representative in having sought to overcome the contradiction. It is, I believe, on this insight that both the force of Marlow's narrative and his interest in Jim depend.

If Kurtz, in *Heart of Darkness,* defines himself by relinquishing his ideals and by rejecting the surface reality that sustained those ideals, Jim defines himself by an opposite response. He relinquishes the truth of experience, the contingency that threatened his confidence in himself on the *Patna,* and molds and defines his reality by an unswerving commitment to the ideal. Moreover, while Kurtz remains essentially anonymous and is inaccessible through his potential capacity for multiple roles, Jim is enigmatic and compelling for Marlow through his steadfast holding of his ideal. Jim may even be characterized as arbitrary and artificial, as a character in a book. Yet he remains closer to Marlow's interest because Jim's reality, though heart-rending, is a moral reality deriving from the code's inflexibility, a reality for which the community has its own share of responsibility.

Marlow is therefore intended by Conrad to provide a principle of authority by which to view Jim as well as the world within which and out of which Jim moves. The structure and narrative of *Lord Jim,* however, do not sustain this principle but rather let it face a confusing reality by which its various constructions begin to lose their solidity. As a consequence, the impressionistic technique that Conrad employs in *Lord Jim* enables him to create and dissolve alternative perspectives. Marlow, for instance, reflects on Jim in order to appropriate the quality of Jim's experience which must remain forever within the area of the inaccessible. For Jim, like Don Quixote, is overdetermined, incapable of conceiving reality realistically. That, however, is precisely the purpose of *Lord Jim:* to question realistic constructions of reality and thereby to bring into view perspectives that would dissolve the boundaries of the familiar. Paradoxically, then, Jim disconnects the link between romantic adventures and books about them on the one hand and his community on the other hand; and he shows the disconnection as a possibility inherent in the very logic of the community's ideals. It is by this paradox that Jim can be comprehended. His initial failure of will ultimately becomes his will to personal authority; failure and success, life and death, become synonymous in Jim's final act on Patusan. This act is martyrdom only from the perspective of his exalted ideal of conduct, for that perspective enfolds within it a common sense perspective that would recognize that act as suicide. The novel thus does not present the two perspectives as alternatives, but rather as mutually implicated views generating an unresolvable textual ambiguity.

Trying to be more than what is permitted by the pragmatic conception of life, Jim must finally take his place as a character in a book, as a fantastic figure of romance, though at the same time for Marlow and for us he also destroys the realistic constructions of reality. Jim consequently construes life itself as a book. Personal authority, however, is something for which there will always be contention between life and book, although a clear answer will be possible only if a clear separation between them is made, and reality separated from illusion. But that cannot be done. Jim is therefore "one of us" through his tragic endeavor to put life and book together. His self-mystification, though inseparable from his tragic failure, is nevertheless the source of his personal authority, whereas Marlow's experience is one of gradual demystification whereby the depth of reality is seen to lie embedded in illusion. *Lord Jim* is thus a story of the transfer of the principle of authority from Marlow, in whom it is at first invested, to Jim, but in traversing the difference between them the real principle of authority that emerges is a questioning of both language and self. For the difference, though it can be imaginatively apprehended, cannot be overcome. Nevertheless, *Lord Jim* would not have its compelling interest for us if Jim did not represent a powerful drive of the human self already implicit in the very tendency of language to invest its concepts with a special ontological status. It is to this tendency that the fundamental tensions which the narrative of *Lord Jim* creates between language and self, ideal and experience can be traced. For these tensions there can be no final response but only narrative beginnings and middles making up the sense of an elusive and contradictory ending.

Lord Jim: Repetition as Subversion of Organic Form

J. Hillis Miller

Lord Jim, like most works of literature, contains self-interpretative elements. Much of it is an explication of words and signs by means of other words, as narrator follows narrator, or as narration is inserted within narration. The critic who attempts to understand *Lord Jim* becomes another in a series of interpreters. He enters into a process of interpretation in which words bring out the meaning of other words and those words refer to others in their turn. No literary text has a manifest pattern, like the design of a rug, which the eye of the critic can survey from the outside and describe as a spatial form, but the intricacies of multiple narrators and time shifts in *Lord Jim* make this particularly evident. The textuality of a text, a "yarn" spun by Conrad, is the meshing of its filaments as they are interwoven in ways hidden from an objectifying eye. The critic must enter into the text, follow its threads as they weave in and out, appearing and disappearing, crisscrossing with other threads. In doing this he adds his own thread of interpretation to the fabric, or he cuts it in one way or another, so becoming part of its texture or changing it. Only in this way can he hope to identify the evasive center or ground which is not visible as a fixed emblem around which the story is spun, but is paradoxically, as Wallace Stevens says in "A Primitive Like an Orb," a "center on the horizon," a center which is outside and around rather than within and punctual.

Samuel Taylor Coleridge, that brilliant manipulator of the met-

From *Fiction and Repetition: Seven English Novels.* © 1982 by the President and Fellows of Harvard College. Harvard University Press, 1982.

aphors of Occidental metaphysics, presents an image of the work of art in its rounded unity corresponding to the assumption that there is such an interior center. Aesthetic wholeness in a narrative, he says, must be copied from the wholeness of a universe which circles in time around the motionless center of a God to whose eternal insight all times are co-present:

> The common end of all *narrative,* nay, of *all,* Poems is to convert a *series* into a *Whole:* to make those events, which in real or imagined History move on in a *strait* line, assume to our Understandings a *circular* motion— the snake with it's Tail in its mouth. Hence indeed the almost flattering and yet appropriate Term, Poesy—i.e. poiesis-*making.* Doubtless, to his eye, which alone comprehends all Past and all Future in one eternal Present, what to our short sight appears strait is but part of the great Cycle—just as the calm Sea to us *appears* level, tho' it indeed [be] only a part of a *globe.* Now what the Globe is in Geography, *miniaturing* in order to *manifest* the Truth, such is a Poem to that Image of God, which we were created with, and which still seeks Unity or Revelation of *One* in and by the *Many.*
>
> (Letter to Joseph Cottle, 1815)

The concept of the organic unity of the work of art, as this passage shows, cannot be detached from its theological basis. Nor can it separate itself from mimetic theories of art. Far from asserting the autonomy of the artwork, its way of being self-sufficiently rounded in on itself, Coleridge here describes the poem as an image or a representation, even the representation of a representation. Its globular roundness miniatures not God in his relation to the creation, but the image of God created in our souls which drives us to seek the one in the many. The poem is the image of an image. Moreover, the oneness revealed in and by the many is not intrinsic but extrinsic. It is the center of a circle made up of a series of events which move in sequence but are curved back on themselves, like the fabled snake with its tail in its mouth, by the attraction of that center, just as the soul "in order to be an individual Being . . . must go forth *from* God, yet as the *receding* from *him* is to *proceed* towards Nothingness and Privation, it must still at every step turn back toward him in order to *be* at all—Now, a straight Line, continuously retracted forms of necessity a circular orbit." The creation, the soul, the work of art—all three have the same shape, the same movement, and the same relation to a generative center. They are related in a descending series of analogical equivalences, each a copy of the one above and all able to be defined by the same geometrical or zoological metaphors.

In place of this kind of doubling, twice removed, of God's universe by the little world of the work of art, Conrad presents for both cosmos and work of literature a structure which has no beginning, no foundation outside itself, and exists only as a self-generated web:

> There is a—let us say—a machine. It evolved itself (I am severely scientific) out of a chaos of scraps of iron and behold!—it knits. I am horrified at the horrible work and stand appalled. I feel it ought to embroider—but it goes on knitting . . . And the most withering thought is that the infamous thing has made itself; made itself without thought, without conscience, without foresight, without eyes, without heart. It is a tragic accident—and it has happened . . . It knits us in and it knits us out. It has knitted time, space, pain, death, corruption, despair and all the illusions—and nothing matters. I'll admit however that to look at the remorseless process is sometimes amusing.
>
> (Letter to R. B. Cunninghame Graham,
> December 20, 1897)

One way of looking at the remorseless process is by way of a novel, but a novel is not for Conrad an *image* of the horrible knitting machine and its work. It is part of the knitting, woven into its web. The infamous machine has made human beings and all their works too, including language and its power of generating or of expressing all the illusions. Works of art, like man's other works, are what they are "in virtue of that truth one and immortal which lurks in the force that made [the machine] spring into existence." Product of the same force which has knit the rest of the universe, a work of art has the same kind of structure. A novel by Conrad, though it invites the reader to hope that he can find a center of the sort Coleridge ascribes to the good work of art, has nothing certainly identifiable outside itself by which it might be measured or from which it might be seen.

It has no visible thematic or structuring principle which will allow the reader to find out its secret, explicate it once and for all, untie all its knots and straighten all its threads. The knitting machine cannot be said to be the origin of the cloth it knits, since what the machine knits is itself, knitter and knitted forming one indistinguishable whole without start or finish, continuously self-creating. The cloth exists as the process of its knitting, the twisting of its yarns as they are looped and knotted by a pervasive "force." This force is the truth one and immortal everywhere present but nowhere visible in itself, an energy both of differentiation and of destruction. "It knits us in and it knits us out."

A familiar passage in Conrad's *Heart of Darkness* describes the indirection characteristic of works of literature like *Lord Jim*. The passage uses a variant of the image of the knitted fabric in the letter to Cunninghame Graham. "The yarns of seamen," says the narrator, "have a direct simplicity, the whole meaning of which lies within the shell of a cracked nut. But Marlow was not typical (if his propensity to spin yarns be excepted), and to him the meaning of an episode was not inside like a kernel but outside, enveloping the tale which brought it out only as a glow brings out a haze, in the likeness of one of those misty halos that sometimes are made visible by the spectral illumination of moonshine." Though the meaning is outside, it may only be seen by way of the tale which brings it out. This bringing out takes place in the interaction of its different elements in their reference to one another. These the critic must track, circling from one word or image to another within the text. Only in this movement of interpretation does the meaning exist. It is not a central and originating node, like the kernel of a nut, a solid and pre-existing nub. It is a darkness, an absence, a haze invisible in itself and only made visible by the ghostlike indirection of a light which is already derived. It is not the direct light of the sun but the reflected light of the moon which brings out the haze. This visible but secondary light and the invisible haze create a halo of "moonshine" which depends for its existence on the reader's involvement in the play of light and dark which generates it. Does this invitation to believe that there is an explanatory center, without positive identification of that center or even certainty about whether or not it exists, in fact characterize *Lord Jim?* I shall investigate briefly here a series of ways the novel might be interpreted.

The theme of *Lord Jim* is stated most explicitly toward the end of chapter 5, in Marlow's attempt to explain why he concerns himself with Jim:

> Why I longed to go grubbing into the deplorable depths of an occurrence which, after all, concerned me no more than as a member of an obscure body of men held together by a community of inglorious toil and by fidelity to a certain standard of conduct, I can't explain. You may call it an unhealthy curiosity if you like; but I have a distinct notion I wished to find something. Perhaps, unconsciously, I hoped I would find that something, some profound and redeeming cause, some merciful explanation, some convincing shadow of an excuse. I see well enough now that I hoped for the impossible—for the laying of what is the most obstinate ghost of man's creation, of the uneasy doubt uprising like a mist, secret and gnawing like a worm, and more chilling than the certitude of death—the doubt of the sovereign power enthroned in a fixed standard of conduct.

Jim is "one of us," an Englishman, son of a country clergyman, a "gentleman," brought up in the British traditions of duty, obedience, quiet faithfulness, and unostentatious courage. Nevertheless, he has committed the shockingly dishonorable act of deserting his ship and the helpless pilgrims it carried. Jim's desertion seems especially deplorable to Marlow because Jim looks so trustworthy, so perfect an example of the unassuming nobility of the tradition from which he has sprung. "He had no business to look so sound," says Marlow. "I thought to myself—well, if this sort can go wrong like that . . . and I felt as though I could fling down my hat and dance on it from sheer mortification"; "He looked as genuine as a new sovereign, but there was some infernal alloy in his metal" (chap. 5). The discrepancy between what Jim looks like and what he is puts in question for Marlow "the sovereign power enthroned in a fixed standard of conduct." He does not doubt the existence of the standard, the seaman's code of fidelity, obedience, and obscure courage on which the British empire was built. He comes to question the power installed behind this standard and within it. This power, as its defining adjective affirms, justifies the standard as its king—its principle, its source, its law.

If there is no sovereign power enthroned in the fixed standard of conduct then the standard is without validity. It is an all-too-human fiction, an arbitrary code of behavior—"this precious notion of a convention," as Marlow says, "only one of the rules of the game, nothing more" (chap. 7). Nothing matters, and anything is possible, as in that condition of spiritual anarchy which takes over on the ship's boat after Jim and the other officers have deserted the *Patna* and left her to sink with eight hundred men, women, and children. "After the ship's lights had gone," says Jim, "anything might have happened in that boat—anything in the world—and the world no wiser. I felt this, and I was pleased. It was just dark enough, too. We were like men walled up quick in a roomy grave. No concern with anything on earth. Nobody to pass an opinion. Nothing mattered . . . No fear, no law, no sounds, no eyes—not even our own, till—till sunrise at least" (chap. 10). Marlow interprets Jim's words in a way which gives them the widest application to the derelict condition of a man who has lost faith, conviction, his customary material surroundings—whatever has given his world stability and order by seeming to support it from outside. "When your ship fails you," says Marlow, "your whole world seems to fail you; the world that made you, restrained you, taken [*sic*] care of you. It is as if the souls of men floating on an abyss and in touch with immensity had been set free for any excess of heroism, absurdity, or abomination. Of course, as with belief, thought, love, hate, conviction, or even the visual aspect of material things, there are as many shipwrecks as there are men . . . Trust a boat on the high seas to bring out the Irrational that lurks at the bottom of every thought, sentiment, sensation, emotion" (chap. 10).

Marlow's aim (or Conrad's) seems clear: to find some explanation for Jim's action which will make it still possible to believe in the sovereign power. Many critics think that in the end Marlow (or Conrad) is satisfied, that even Jim is satisfied. The circumstances of Jim's death and his willingness to take responsibility for the death of Dain Waris ("He hath taken it upon his own head"; chap. 45) make up for all Jim has done before. Jim's end re-enthrones the regal power justifying the fixed standard of conduct by which he condemns himself to death.

Matters are not so simple in this novel. For one thing, there is something suspect in Marlow's enterprise of interpretation. "Was it for my own sake," he asks, "that I wished to find some shadow of an excuse for that young fellow whom I had never seen before?"

(chap. 5). If so much is at stake for himself, he is likely to find what he wants to find.

Marlow attempts to maintain his faith in the sovereign power in several contradictory ways. One is to discover that there are extenuating circumstances. Perhaps Jim is not all bad. Perhaps he can be excused. Perhaps he can ultimately redeem himself. At other times Marlow suggests that in spite of appearances Jim has a fatal soft spot. He cannot be safely trusted for an instant. If this is so, then he must be condemned in the name of the kingly law determining good and evil, praise and blame. At still other times Marlow's language implies that Jim is the victim of dark powers within himself, powers which also secretly govern the universe outside. If there is no benign sovereign power there may be a malign one, a principle not of light but of blackness, "a destructive fate ready for us all" (chap. 5). If this is the case, there are indeed extenuating circumstances, precisely the "shadow of an excuse." To act according to a fixed standard of conduct which is justified by no sovereign power, as perhaps Jim does in his death, is the truest heroism. It is defiance of the shadowy powers which would undermine everything man finds good. If this is so, Jim's death is nevertheless in one sense still a sham. It is a sham in the sense that it is valued by no extrahuman judge. It is only one way of acting among others.

Perhaps, to pursue this line a little further, the source of all Jim's trouble is his romanticism, that childish image of himself as a hero which has its source in fraudulent literature and sticks with him all his life: "He confronted savages on tropical shores, quelled mutinies on the high seas, and in a small boat upon the ocean kept up the hearts of despairing men—always an example of devotion to duty, and as unflinching as a hero in a book" (chap. 1). Perhaps it is Jim's confidence in this illusory image of himself which is the source of his inability to confront the truth about himself and about the universe. Perhaps this confidence even paradoxically explains his repeated acts of cowardice. It may be that Jim's death is no more than the last of such acts, his last failure to face the dark side of himself which is so rudely brought back before him in the person of Gentleman Brown. His death may be no more than his last attempt to act according to a fictional idea of heroic conduct. Certainly the final paragraphs of the novel show Marlow by no means "satisfied." The ending is a tissue of unanswered questions in which Marlow affirms once more not that Jim is a hero or that Jim is a coward, but that he remains an indecipherable mystery:

> And that's the end. He passes away under a cloud, inscrutable at heart, forgotten, unforgiven, and excessively romantic . . . He goes away from a living woman to celebrate his pitiless wedding with a shadowy ideal of conduct. Is he satisfied—quite, now, I wonder? We ought to know. He is one of us—and have I not stood up once, like an evoked ghost, to answer for his eternal constancy? Was I so very wrong after all? Now he is no more, there are days when the reality of his existence comes to me with an immense, with an overwhelming force; and yet upon my honour there are moments, too, when he passes from my eyes like a disembodied spirit astray amongst the passions of this earth, ready to surrender himself faithfully to the claim of his own world of shades.
>   Who knows?
>
> (chap. 45)

The ending seems to confirm Marlow's earlier statement that the heart of each man is a dark forest to all his fellows and "loneliness" a "hard and absolute condition of existence": "The envelope of flesh and blood on which our eyes are fixed melts before the outstretched hand, and there remains only the capricious, unconsolable, and elusive spirit that no eye can follow, no hand can grasp" (chap. 16).

On the other hand, all that seems problematic and inconclusive about Lord Jim when it is approached from the point of view of explicit thematic statements and by way of Marlow's interpretation of Jim may be resolved if the reader stands back from Marlow's perspective and looks at the novel as a whole. The detached view may see the truth, according to that proverb Marlow recalls which affirms that "the onlookers see most of the game" (chap. 21). Seen from a distance, Lord Jim may turn out to be a pattern of recurrent motifs which reveals more about Jim than Marlow comes to understand. Jim's feeling at his trial that "only a meticulous precision of statement would bring out the true horror behind the face of things" (chap. 4) may be the clue to the aesthetic method of the book. The episodes Marlow and others relate, the language they use, may reveal to the readers of the novel a secret hidden from Marlow, from Jim, and from all the characters, a secret known only to Conrad. He may have chosen this way to show forth the truth because only as a participant in its revelation can the reader understand it.

When *Lord Jim* is approached from the perspective of its narrative structure and its design of recurrent images it reveals itself to be not less but more problematic, more inscrutable, like Jim himself. I have elsewhere argued that temporal form, interpersonal relations, and relations of fiction and reality are three structuring principles fundamental to fiction. *Lord Jim* is an admirable example of the tendency of these in their interaction to weave a fabric of words which is incapable of being interpreted unambiguously, as a fixed pattern of meaning, even though the various possibilities of meaning are rigorously delimited by the text.

To begin with the structure of interpersonal relations: Victorian novels were often apparently stabilized by the presence of an omniscient narrator, spokesman for the collective wisdom of the community, though, as my Victorian examples [elsewhere] demonstrate, such a narrator never turns out to be unequivocally the basis of the storytelling when a given Victorian novel is interpreted in detail. Such a narrator, if he were ever to exist, would represent a trustworthy point of view and also a safe vantage point from which to watch the hearts and minds of the characters in their relations to one another. Conrad, as many critics have noted, does not employ a "reliable" narrator. In *Lord Jim* no point of view is entirely trustworthy. The novel is a complex design of interrelated minds, no one of which can be taken as a secure point of reference from which the others may be judged.

The first part of the story is told by an "omniscient" narrator who seems like the narrator of a novel by Trollope or by George Eliot. This first narrator of *Lord Jim* has the same superhuman powers of insight, including direct access to the hero's mind, that is possessed by those earlier Victorian narrators. He relinquishes that access early in the story, as though it could not provide a satisfactory avenue to the truth behind Jim's life. He then returns in chapter 36, after Marlow's narrative to his almost silent auditors is over. He returns to introduce the man who receives the letter which is Marlow's "last word" about Jim. The bulk of the novel is made up of Marlow's telling of Jim's story to the group of listeners in the darkness who are the reader's surrogates. Those listeners stand between the reader and Marlow's telling. "He existed for me," says Marlow, "and after all it is only through me that he exists for you. I've led him out by the hand; I have paraded him before you" (chap. 21).

Many sections of the story are told to Marlow by Jim. In these the reader can see Jim attempting to interpret his experience by putting it into words. This self-interpretation is interpreted once more by Marlow, then by implication interpreted again by Marlow's listeners. The latter appear occasionally as intervening minds, as when one of them says: "You are so subtle, Marlow" (chap. 8). This overlapping of interpretative minds within minds is put in question in its turn, at least implicitly, by the "omniscient" narrator. He surrounds all and perhaps understands all, though he does not give the reader the sort of interpretative help provided by the narrator of *Middlemarch* or of *The Last Chronicle of Barset.* Even so, this narrator may have been brought back briefly near the end of the novel to suggest that the reader might be wise to put in question Marlow's interpretation of Jim, even though the narrator cannot or will not provide the reader with any solid alternative ground on which to stand.

Within Marlow's narrative there are many minor characters—Captain Brierly, the French lieutenant, Chester, Stein—who have their say in the story. They are irreplaceable points of view on Jim within Marlow's point of view. They are sources of parts of his story and offer alternative ways of judging it. Their own stories, moreover, are analogous to Jim's story, though whether in a positive or in a negative way is often hard to tell. Just as the crucial episodes in Jim's life echo one another, the jump from the *Patna* repeating his failure to jump in the small boat when he was in training and being repeated again by his jump over the stockade in Patusan ("Patusan" recalling *Patna*), so Captain Brierly's suicide is a jump ambiguously duplicating Jim's jumps (was it cowardly or an act of heroism following logically from a shattering insight into the truth of things?), while the French lieutenant's courage shows what Jim might have done on the *Patna,* and Stein's strange history echoes Jim's either positively or negatively. Stein appears to be either an unreliable narrator or a trustworthy commentator, depending on one's judgment of his life and personality. Is he a man who has bravely immersed himself in the destructive element to win an ultimate wisdom, or has he withdrawn passively from life to collect his butterflies and to give

Marlow and the readers of the novel only misleading clues to the meaning of Jim's life?

Lord Jim is made up of episodes similar in design. In each a man confronts a crisis testing his courage, the strength of his faith in the sovereign power enthroned in a fixed standard of conduct. In each case someone, the man himself or someone else, interprets that test, or rather he interprets the words which the man's reaction to the test has already generated. There is even a parody of this pattern early in the novel, as if to call attention to it as a structuring principle or as a universal way in which men are related to one another. Just as Marlow seeks out the chief engineer of the *Patna* in the hospital "in the eccentric hope of hearing something explanatory of the famous affair from his point of view," so the doctor who is tending the engineer after his brandy debauch says he "never remember[s] being so interested in a case of the jim-jams before." "The head, ah! the head, of course, gone, but the curious part is that there is some sort of method in his raving. I am trying to find out. Most unusual—that thread of logic in such a delirium" (chap. 5). The reader of *Lord Jim*, like the doctor, must seek the thread of logic within a bewildering complexity of words. With these words Conrad attempts to express a truth beyond direct expression in words, "for words also belong to the sheltering conception of light and order which is our refuge" (chap. 33), our refuge from the truth hidden in the darkness. In the sequence of discrete episodes which makes up the novel, no episode serves as the point of origin, the arch-example of the *mythos* of the novel, but each is, by reason of its analogy to other episodes, a repetition of them, each example being as enigmatic as all the others.

A similar complexity characterizes the temporal structure of the novel. Jim says of his memory of watching the other officers struggle to get the *Patna*'s boat in the water: "I ought to have a merry life of it, by God! for I shall see that funny sight a good many times yet before I die" (chap. 9). Of an earlier moment before the officers desert the ship he says: "It was as though I had heard it all, seen it all, gone through it all twenty times already" (chap. 8). Each enactment of a given episode echoes backward and forward indefinitely, creating a pattern of eddying repetition. If there are narrators within narrators there are also times within times—time-shifts, breaks in time, anticipations, retrogressions, retellings, and reminders that a given part of the story has often been told before. Marlow, for example, like the Ancient Mariner, has related Jim's story "many times, in distant parts of the world" (chap. 4). The novel is made up of recurrences in which each part of the story has already happened repeatedly when the reader first encounters it, either in someone's mind, or in someone's telling, or in the way it repeats other similar events in the same person's life or in the lives of others. The temporal structure of the novel is open. *Lord Jim* is a chain of repetitions, each event referring back to others which it both explains and is explained by, while at the same time it prefigures those which will occur in the future. Each exists as part of an infinite regression and progression within which the narrator moves back and forth discontinuously across time seeking unsuccessfully some motionless point in its flow.

It might be argued that the sequence of events as the reader is given them by Conrad, in a deliberately chosen order, is a linear series with a beginning, middle, and end which determines a straightforward development of gradually revealed meaning moving through time as the reader follows word after word and page after page, becoming more and more absorbed in the story and more and more emotionally involved in it. This sequence, it might be argued, generates a determinate meaning. It is true that this linear sequence is shared by any reader and that it establishes a large background of agreement about what happens and even about the meaning of what happens. That Jim jumps from the *Patna* and that this is a morally deplorable act no reader is likely to doubt. But it is also true that the linear sequence of episodes as it is presented to the reader by the various narrators is radically rearranged from the chronological order in which the events actually occurred. This could imply that Conrad, the "omniscient narrator," or Marlow has ordered the episodes in such a way that the best understanding by the reader of a total meaning possessed by one or another of these narrators will be revealed. Or it may imply, as I think it does, that the deeper explanatory meaning behind those facts open to the sunlight, about which anyone would agree, remains hidden, so that any conceivable narrator of these facts or interpreter of them is forced to move back and forth across the facts, putting them in one or another achronological order in the hope that this deeper meaning will reveal itself. The narration in many ways, not least by calling attention to the way one episode repeats another rather than being clearly a temporal advance on it, breaks down the chronological sequence and invites the reader to think of it as a simultaneous set of echoing episodes spread out spatially like villages or mountain peaks on a map. *Lord Jim* too, to borrow the splendid phrase Henry James uses in his review of Conrad's *Chance,* is "a prolonged hovering flight of the subjective over the outstretched ground of the case exposed." Insofar as the novel is this and not the straightforward historical movement suggested by Aristotle's comments on beginning, middle, and end in the *Poetics,* then the sort of metaphysical certainty implicit in Aristotle, the confidence that some *logos* or underlying cause and ground supports the events, is suspended. It is replaced by the image of a consciousness attempting to grope its way to the hidden cause behind a set of enigmatic facts by moving back and forth over them. If the "facts" are determinate (more or less) the novel encourages the reader to seek the "why" behind the events, some "shadow of an excuse." It is here, I am arguing, that the text does not permit the reader to decide among alternative possibilities, even though those possibilities themselves are identified with precise determinate certainty.

The similarities between one episode and another or one character and another in *Lord Jim* no doubt appear to be deliberately designed (whether by Conrad or by Marlow), like most of the cases of repetition discussed [elsewhere]. Such repetitions differ from those which are accidental or merely contingent, perhaps even insignificant, although the reader would do well not to be too sure about the existence of insignificant similarities. Moreover, the fact that Conrad probably consciously intended most of the repetitions I discuss here (though certainty about that is of course impossible) may be trivial compared to the way the novel represents human life as happening to fall into repetitive patterns, whether in the life of a single person, as Jim repeats variants of the same actions over and over, or from person to person, as Brierly's jump repeats Jim's jump. The question the novel asks and cannot unequivocally answer is "Why is this?" To say it is because Conrad designed his novel in recurring patterns is to trivialize the question and to give a misplaced answer to it.

Nor can the meaning of the novel be identified by returning to its historical sources, however helpful or even essential these are in establishing a context for our reading. The "source" of *Lord Jim,* as Conrad tells the reader in the Author's Note, was a glimpse of the "real" Jim: "One sunny morning in the commonplace surroundings of an Eastern roadstead, I saw his form pass by—appealing—significant—under a cloud—perfectly silent . . . It was for me, with all the sympathy of which I was capable, to seek fit words for his meaning." Norman Sherry, in *Conrad's Eastern World,* and Ian Watt, in

Conrad in the Nineteenth Century, have discussed in detail the historical events which lie behind the novel. *Lord Jim* can be defined as an attempt on Conrad's part to understand the real by way of a long detour through the fictive. To think of *Lord Jim* as the interpretation of history is to recognize that the historical events "behind" the novel exist now as documents, and that these documents too are enigmatic. They are as interesting for the ways in which Conrad changed them as for the ways in which he repeated them exactly. The novel is related to its sources in a pattern of similarity and difference like that of the episodes inside the novel proper. The facts brought to light by Sherry and Watt, for example the "Report of a Court of Inquiry held at Aden into the cause of the abandonment of the steamship 'Jeddah,' " do not serve as a solid and unequivocal point of origin by means of which the novel may be viewed, measured, and understood. The documents are themselves mysterious, as mysterious as the Old Yellow Book on which Browning based *The Ring and the Book* or as the dry, factual account of historical events included at the end of Melville's *Benito Cereno.* In all these cases knowledge of the historical sources makes the story based on them not less but more inscrutable, more difficult to understand. If there are "fit words" for Jim's "meaning" they are to be found only within the novel, not in any texts outside it.

Perhaps, to turn to a last place where an unambiguous meaning may be found, the pattern of images in its recurrences somehow transcends the complexities I have discussed. It may constitute a design lying in the sunlight, ready to be seen and understood. It will be remembered that Conrad attempts above all, as he says in the preface to *The Nigger of the "Narcissus,"* to make us *see.* Matching this is the recurrent image in *Lord Jim* according to which Marlow gets glimpses of Jim through a rift in the clouds. "The views he let me have of himself," says Marlow, "were like those glimpses through the shifting rents in a thick fog—bits of vivid and vanishing detail, giving no connected idea of the general aspect of a country" (chap. 6). The metaphorical structure of the novel may reveal in such disconnected glimpses a secret which cannot be found out by exploring its narrative, temporal, or interpersonal patterns, or by extracting explicit thematic statements.

A network of light and dark imagery manifestly organizes the novel throughout. It is first established insistently near the beginning in the description of the *Patna* steaming across the calm sea: "The

Patna, with a slight hiss, passed over that plain luminous and smooth, unrolled a black ribbon of smoke across the sky, left behind her on the water a white ribbon of foam that vanished at once, like the phantom of a track drawn upon a lifeless sea by the phantom of a steamer" (chap. 2). Black against white, light against dark—perhaps the meaning of *Lord Jim* is to be found in Conrad's manipulation of this binary pattern.

This metaphorical or "symbolic" pattern too is systematically ambiguous, as may be seen by looking at two examples, the description of Jim's visit to Marlow's room after his trial and the description of Marlow's last glimpse of Jim on the shore. The juxtaposition of light and dark offers no better standing ground from which what is equivocal about the rest of the novel may be surveyed and comprehended than any other aspect of the text. The "visual aspect of material things" and the clues it may offer to the meaning of man's life sink in the general shipwreck which puts in doubt the sovereign power enthroned in a fixed standard of conduct:

> He remained outside, faintly lighted on the background of night, as if standing on the shore of a sombre and hopeless sea.
>
> An abrupt heavy rumble made me lift my head. The noise seemed to roll away, and suddenly a searching and violent glare fell on the blind face of the night. The sustained and dazzling flickers seemed to last for an unconscionable time. The growl of the thunder increased steadily while I looked at him, distinct and black, planted solidly upon the shores of a sea of light. At the moment of greatest brilliance the darkness leaped back with a culminating crash, and he vanished before my dazzled eyes as utterly as though he had been blown to atoms.
>
> (chap. 16)

> He was white from head to foot, and remained persistently visible with the stronghold of the night at his back, the sea at his feet, the opportunity by his side—still veiled. What do you say? Was it still veiled? I don't know. For me that white figure in the stillness of coast and sea seemed to stand at the heart of a vast enigma. The twilight was ebbing fast from the sky above his head, the strip of sand had sunk already under his feet, he himself appeared no bigger

than a child—then only a speck, a tiny white speck, that
seemed to catch all the light left in a darkened world . . .
And, suddenly, I lost him.

(chap. 35)

In one of these passages Jim is the light that illuminates the
darkness. In the other he is the blackness that stands out against a
blinding light which suddenly reveals itself from its hiding place and
then disappears. Light changes place with dark; the value placed on
dark and light changes place, as light is sometimes the origin of dark,
dark sometimes the origin of light. Each such passage, moreover,
refers to the others by way of anticipation or recollection, as the first
of the texts quoted prefigures the second, but when the reader turns
to the other passage it is no easier to understand and itself refers to
other such passages. No one of them is the original ground, the basis
on which the others may be interpreted. *Lord Jim* is like a dictionary
in which the entry under one word refers the reader to another word
which refers him to another and then back to the first word again, in
an endless circling. Marlow sitting in his hotel room ceaselessly writing letters by the light of a single candle while Jim struggles with his
conscience and the thunderstorm prepares in the darkness outside
may be taken as an emblem of literature as Conrad sees it. A work
of literature is for him in a paradoxical relation to a nonverbal reality
it seeks both to uncover and to evade in the creation of its own
exclusively verbal realm.

I claim, then, that from whatever angle it is approached *Lord Jim*
reveals itself to be a work which raises questions rather than answer-
ing them. The fact that it contains its own interpretations does not
make it easier to understand. The overabundance of possible explanations only inveigles the reader to share in the self-sustaining motion of a process of interpretation which cannot reach an unequivocal
conclusion. This weaving movement of advance and retreat constitutes and sustains the meaning of the text, that evasive center which
is everywhere and nowhere in the play of its language.

Marlow several times calls explicit attention to the unendingness
of the process by which he and the readers of the novel go over and
over the details of Jim's life in an ever-renewed, never-successful
attempt to understand it completely and so write "Finis" to his story.
"And besides," affirms Marlow apropos of his "last" words about
Jim, "the last word is not said,—probably shall never be said. Are

not our lives too short for that full utterance which through all our stammerings is of course our only and abiding intention? . . . There is never time to say our last word—the last word of our love, or our desire, faith, remorse, submission, revolt" (chap. 21). The reader will remember here those "last words" of Kurtz ("The horror! The horror!") which Marlow in another story hears and ironically praises for their finality, their power to sum up. If this theme is repeated within *Lord Jim,* these repetitions echo in their turn passages in other novels by Conrad. If *Heart of Darkness* leads to Marlow's recognition that he cannot understand Kurtz as long as he has not followed Kurtz all the way into the abyss of death, the "ending" of *Lord Jim* is Marlow's realization that it is impossible to write "The End" to any story: "End! Finis! the potent word that exorcises from the house of life the haunting shadow of fate. This is what—notwithstanding the testimony of my eyes and his own earnest assurances—I miss when I look back upon Jim's success. While there's life there is hope, truly; but there is fear, too . . . he made so much of his disgrace while it is the guilt alone that matters. He was not—if I may say so—clear to me. He was not clear. And there is a suspicion he was not clear to himself either" (chap. 16). Nor can he, I am arguing, ever be clear to us, except with the paradoxical clarity generated by our recognition that the process of interpreting his story is a ceaseless movement toward a light which always remains hidden in the dark.

Let there be no misunderstanding here. The situation I have just described does not mean that the set of possible explanations for Jim's action is limitless, indeterminate in the sense of being indefinitely multiple and nebulous. The various meanings are not the free imposition of subjective interpretations by the reader, but are controlled by the text. In that sense they are determinate. The novel provides the textual material for identifying exactly what the possible explanations are. The reader is not permitted to go outside the text to make up other possible explanations of his own. The indeterminacy lies in the multiplicity of possible incompatible explanations given by the novel and in the lack of evidence justifying a choice of one over the others. The reader cannot logically have them all, and yet nothing he is given determines a choice among them. The possibilities, moreover, are not just given side by side as entirely separate hypotheses. They are related to one another in a system of mutual implication and mutual contradiction. Each calls up the others, but it does not make sense to have more than one of them.

Lord Jim: Destruction through Time

Daniel Cottom

> *O goodly golden chaine, wherewith yfere*
> *The vertues linked are in louely wize:*
> *And noble minds of yore allyed were,*
> *On braue poursuit of cheualrous emprize,*
> *That none did others safety despize,*
> *Nor aid enuy to him, in need that stands,*
> *But friendly each did others prayse deuise*
> *How to aduance with fauourable hands.*
> —SPENSER

According to *Lord Jim*, to be too sensitive for this world is to assume that there exists a different world to which one properly belongs and for the sake of which one suffers. Although this suffering may acquire an exemplary significance if it reflects the myths of society at large, in the absence of this reference it comes to signify a narcissistic attitude that is not only without social value but also positively inimical to society. At best, this suffering may be perceived as " 'a sort of sublimated, idealised selfishness' " akin to the quality of self-indulgence that Conrad attributed to Don Quixote, adding that the knight "was not a good citizen." Such is the situation of Jim as the modern world of Conrad's novel is distinguished from the past by

From *The Centennial Review* 27, no. 1 (Winter 1983). © 1983 by *The Centennial Review*.

the way that it redefines sensitivity and sacrifice as dishonor and disillusionment. In a world that no longer sanctions otherworldly belief as the basis for interpreting behavior, the demonic individual is not he who revolts from the position of faith but rather the individual who, like Jim, clings to it above all else. In effect, Jim loses his honor because the world has lost its capacity to nuture this quality. He fails to be a hero because the world is no longer a world of heroism, or at least of such heroism as that in which he puts his faith. He is brought low and chased to the ends of the earth by the deadly power of a dead rhetoric.

Unwilling to commit himself to anything short of absolute truth, Jim commits himself only to an unilluminating death. Driven to objectify his desire in an exemplary form, Jim succeeds only in exemplifying failure. As the anonymous narrator of the beginning of the novel describes Jim's project, the deadly spirit that causes this failure is introduced:

> After his first feeling of revolt he had come round to the view that only a meticulous precision of statement would bring out the true horror behind the appalling face of things. The facts those men were so eager to know had been visible, tangible, open to the senses . . . they made a whole that had features, shades of expression, a complicated aspect that could be remembered by the eye, and something else besides, something invisible, a directing spirit of perdition that dwelt within, like a malevolent soul in a detestable body. He was anxious to make this clear.

This "malevolent soul" is the perverted spirit of the mythical past with which Jim identifies, and he will never be able to make it clear because it can have no reality for those who do not have his attachment to this outmoded world. Jim's problem is that his anxious desire places him outside the secular morality characteristic of late nineteenth-century society even though it places him in the symbolic tradition central to that society. What Marlow describes and sympathetically suffers through the character of Jim is the disparity between the necessary enforcement of a moral code, on the one hand, and, on the other, the absence in the modern world of the transcendent belief traditionally presumed to be the basis of that code. Jim suffers from this internal contradiction in the modern world—this rhetorical lip-service to and practical denial of its mythical background—because he is not subtle enough to catch that cynical materialism which is the unmentionable assumption of modernity here as throughout Conrad's fiction. In the modern world, at least, Jacques Berthoud is right in saying that "taken to its logical conclusion, honour becomes absolutely incompatible with life." In other words, Jim's problem is his inability to understand that in the modern world one must suffer without otherworldly motivation or redemption.

Paul L. Wiley has described this situation as follows:

> The imaginary realm, timeless and ordered, in which Jim dreams of himself as a hero and a savior contains values and fine judgments on the score of conduct which stem from a chivalric and religious tradition. . . . He wants specifically to be a Christian hero, to give his life for others if need be, and the irony of his story . . . lies in the fact that this attempt to transcend the brutality of existence involves him ever more deeply in the toils of a universe offering no support for such a dream.
>
> (*Conrad's Measure of Man*)

The irony goes still further, however. In fact, it goes so far in this novel as to leave no response to Jim's self-destructive narcissism except an equally destructive commitment to the repression of one's self and the oppression of others. The "spirit of perdition" that haunts Jim and that he is unable to make clear is also Jim himself as Marlow is haunted by him and unable to see him clearly. Thus the tale of Jim's fate also serves to reveal the demonic soul of the community from which Jim is exiled and with which Marlow identifies. Jim is, as it were, the neurotic symptom that takes form on the body of modern Western civilization because of the irresoluble contradiction internal to it. Marlow's repeated assertion that Jim is " 'one of us' " is as much a curse as it is a statement of sympathy. If Jim's problem is that he is unable to understand the absence of spirituality in the modern world and so never ceases to be haunted by this absence, the problem of the community that Marlow represents is that it is unable to admit the insubstantiality of the secular values with which it has replaced spirituality and so never ceases to be haunted by illusions that are, if anything, more pathetic and more deadly than Jim's.

II

In order to create the life he desires—that is, a life that would objectify his desires—Jim would have to be a modern magician. He needs magical powers because the role he wants to play is the ideal role of the knight, and such a figure needs magical powers in order to overcome the endlessly challenging temporality to which he is bound. As Angus Fletcher has written in reference to Spenser,

> The typical knight of *The Faerie Queen* has always a further trial ahead of him, and, as numerous critics have noted, the reward for victory in one battle or progress is always a new challenge. There is no such thing as satisfaction in this world; daemonic agency implies a *manie de perfection,* an impossible desire to become one with an image of unchanging purity.
>
> *(Allegory: The Theory of a Symbolic Mode)*

Continuous commitment and continuous action are essential to the knight. If he pauses for even a moment, he fails. As Erich Auerbach put it,

> Except feats of arms and love, nothing can occur in the courtly world—and even these two are of a special sort; they are not occurrences or emotions which can be absent for a time; they are permanently connected with the person of the perfect knight, they are part of his definition, so that he cannot for one moment be without adventure in arms nor for one moment without amorous entanglement.
>
> *(Mimesis: The Representation of Reality in Western Literature,* trans. Willard R. Trask)

And yet, paradoxically, it is this entanglement in arms and love that the knight really seeks to conquer. His goal is always transcendent, and this transcendent goal is to preserve the particular scene of victory as a lasting worldly incarnation of spiritual truth. Through his continuous action, the knight wants to put a stop to time; the endlessness of his engagements bespeaks the desired eternity. Although such a project may be possible in a mythical universe, however, *Lord Jim* dramatizes its desperate inappropriateness to the modern world in terms of a general failure of action and language that seek revelation.

According to *Lord Jim,* the classificatory orders presupposed by magical thought that is believed and lived—those golden chains of resemblances, analogies, correspondences, and hierarchies that bring everything in the universe into harmony—become secularized in modern thought into interpretative procedures and strategies presumptive of nothing but the pragmatic necessity of establishing control in an otherwise inchoate community. An ontological ground for morality is simply out of the question. Marlow says, " 'The real significance of crime is in its being a breach of faith with the community of mankind,' " and his grafting of secular values to religious rhetoric in this passage shows the cultural contradiction with which Jim must contend. Marlow's words are baseless. The world is bereft of transcendence, and humanity is no substitute for it. In the modern world of Conrad's novel humanity cannot have the quasi-divine status that it sometimes could, say, in the novels of George Eliot. Lacking a sacred order of any sort, then, the modern magician can only base his actions upon the ordinary needs of social governance, and an abject and illusory magic is all that can result from this subjection to profane authority.

Even words, as Marlow says, " 'belong to the sheltering conception of light and order which is our refuge.' " Like actions, words serve only to deflect truth rather than to reflect or incarnate it. When magic thus becomes a form of defensive servility rather than a way to transcendent knowledge, bathos becomes the emotional, melodrama the theatrical, convention the social, and cliché the linguistic form that human relationships must assume. Marlow's tale moves throughout such registers as it seeks to material ize its subject, but " 'there remains only the capricious, unconsolable, and elusive spirit that no eye can follow, no hand can grasp.' " A character whose essence is his romantic commitment to an ideal is simply impossible to understand in a modern text to which such idealism is essentially foreign.

For Marlow regarding Jim as for Jim regarding the world, then, there is always this unreachable and threatening agent behind appearances, like that sinister will which sometimes appears to the mariner, meaning "to sweep the whole precious world utterly away from his sight by the simple and appalling act of taking his life." To those who do not recognize the death of spiritual reality, its legacy is the transformation of the universe into a demonic conspiracy against them, while its legacy to those who recognize its passing while still maintaining a superficial allegiance to it is their bedevilment by characters who, like Jim, are quite literally too good to be real and thus, paradoxically, not good enough. Jim's very belief in goodness is an evil in the modern world, and yet Marlow's cynicism cannot protect him from being haunted by Jim because he recognizes that secular codes of speech and action are also fundamentally baseless illusions, or hapless magic.

In the mist and the veil and the fog that distance Jim from Marlow and from the reader, in the capricious workings of a language in which " 'the power of sentences has nothing to do with their sense or the logic of their construction,' " in the unpredictable wounding and the unpredictable strength of the *Patna,* and in love above all else, this ghost of a dead spirituality haunts " 'the forlorn magicians that we are.' " Failure is inevitably the common fate, as Marlow recognizes when he says of Jim, " 'no magician's wand can immobilize him under my eyes.' " The superhuman power that compels this human failure, however, is absent and unnameable. Or, to put it in other words, it is absence itself, the erosion of meaning through the course of history that leaves behind it an empty and therefore destructive rhetoric. At best one can only evoke this daunting power tangentially by pointing to the words, objects, or characters that happen to appear contiguous to an event. They may be empty facts, but they are all that there is to go on in the modern world. As Marlow says of Cornelius, the apparent cause of Jim's death, " 'He has his place neither in the background nor in the foreground of the story; he is simply seen skulking on its outskirts, enigmatical and unclean, tainting the fragrance of its youth and of its naiveness.' " Failure is, as it were, the underlying premise of the modern universe, so that the search for a specific cause of failure and the attempt to transcend failure are equally anachronistic and equally impossible tasks, and both in equal measure tragic and ludicrous. Thus, it is Jim's obstinate refusal to acknowledge this unnameable power that condemns him. As Edward Crankshaw has remarked, "The whole problem about Jim is that he never does lose his self-respect."

As he talks about his first encounter with Patusan and Jim's beloved, Marlow describes the form taken in this foreign land by " 'this amazing Jim-myth' " which is also his subject. The passage is worth quoting at length, for the difference between the native myth and Marlow's story displays in miniature the disjunction between mythical and modern consciousness that is the source of the tragedy, the repulsive comedy, and the ultimate futility of the position Jim tries to assume towards the world. Marlow says,

> Jim called her by a word that means precious, in the sense of a precious gem—jewel. . . . I was struck by the name, of course; but it was not till later on that I connected it with an astonishing rumour that had met me on my journey. . . . I discovered that a story was travelling slowly down the coast about a mysterious white man in Patusan who had got hold of an extraordinary gem—namely, an emerald of an enormous size, and altogether priceless. The emerald seems to appeal more to the Eastern imagination than any other precious stone. The white man had obtained it, I was told, partly by the exercise of his wonderful strength and partly by cunning, from the ruler of a distant country, whence he had fled instantly, arriving in Patusan in utmost distress, but frightening the people by his extreme ferocity, which nothing seemed able to subdue. Most of my informants were of the opinion that the stone was probably unlucky—like the famous stone of the Sultan of Succadana, which in the old times had brought wars and untold calamities upon that country. Perhaps it was the same stone—one couldn't say. Indeed the story of a fabulously large emerald is as old as the arrival of the first white men in the Archipelago. . . . such a jewel—it was explained to me by the old fellow . . . is best preserved by being concealed about the person of a woman.

Although the creation of this myth might seem to show that in Patusan Jim has found a realm appropriate to him, one that will nurture his romantic character, the irony is that it undercuts his idealism as much as the process of the law-court had. As it takes literally the metaphorical association by which Jim had named his beloved so as to picture that woman as one used to hide a fantastic jewel, the myth can be seen to mock the romantic idealism with which Jim regards her. She is not so much a real woman to him as she is a metaphor, a figure whom he can invest with his illusions, depending upon her to protect them. The distortion of Jim's metaphor as it is taken up by the native myth, then, foretells the failure of his desire to regard human beings and earthly occasions as if they really could be jewels: fabulous, pure, ideally beautiful, everlasting.

The distortion of metaphor evident in this confusion of signifier and signified perfectly exemplifies the way that Jim is captive to a rhetoric of knightly ideality that has lost its semantic ground in the world and therefore dooms Jim to be misperceived, misjudged, and mistrusted by others. And, of course, not only does Jim suffer from outworn metaphor, but he himself becomes a corrupt metaphor: *Tuan* Jim, Lord Jim.

Even myth betrays Jim, then, although it betrays him only by implicitly foretelling the fact that Jim will fail as a knight and will betray his idealistic commitment to Jewel even as he suicidally fulfills himself as a knight of arms. This knightly code that has descended to Jim beyond its appropriate cultural ground by way of "a course of light holiday literature" is the spirit that he will never be able to materialize in a coherent fashion because it no longer has any material significance. The Jim-myth, then, may bear some resemblance to the story in the medieval *Pearl;* both stories may involve an obsessive concern with purity and flawlessness, a gem that is also a maiden and a possible salvation, a narrator who is educated in the course of the story, and an oneiric setting; but these similarities serve only to emphasize the difference between the faith underlying the medieval text and the cynicism that dominates Marlow's tale.

Jim cannot hide from his past in Patusan or anywhere else for the same reason that the name of his lover, which " 'he would say . . . as he might have said "Jane," ' " cannot be kept from an exotic distortion of its intended meaning as it is voiced by others. Although, as Paul Kirschner has suggested, Jim "regards his own conduct as a performance, for which he needs a suitable stage," he is unable to find that stage because he is unable to dissociate himself from the world into which he was born. Like Marlow in his narration, Jim in his life is unable to materialize a self-fulfilling stage that is not seen " 'through the eyes of others.' " The natives of Patusan may live in myth— though even on its own terms their world appears far from ideal—but Jim is bound to the modern stage of Western history.

All that Jim wants is " ' "some sort of chance" ' " that he calls a " ' "clean slate." ' " He thinks he ought to be given a moment of exalted opportunity that would spring upon him like James's "beast in the jungle." He wants the ultimate victory of the knight, that transcendent satisfaction which Royal Roussel has described as "that self-completing action which is the object of his adventure." But even though Jim thinks that Marlow has given him this chance with the introduction to Stein and thence to Patusan, Marlow says, " 'I remain strangely unenlightened.' " What Marlow recognizes is that the idea of a liberating chance is excluded from "the distinction of being white" and therefore is as vulnerable as " 'the smooth face of a rock' " that Captain Brierly presents to the world even as he prepares to kill himself. This idea belongs to the world clustered around concepts like *miracle, romance, spirit, imagination,* and *exultation,* a world with which Marlow continually flirts but which he must reject so that he can distinguish himself from Jim by identifying with the world clustered around concepts like *control, subjugation, duty, conduct,* and *law.* The Enlightenment rationalism, recalled by the image of the clean slate, and the post-Enlightenment Romanticism, recalled by the world of myth in this novel, are both of a type so far as the stage of the modern world is concerned; for both imply the possibility of a dissociation from the path that history has taken. A vision of apocalyptic change may be available in *The Pearl,* but Jim cannot find this moment that would upset history and put an end to time.

III

For the modern knight, it is only through unhesitating and unending action that a belief in transcendent freedom can be supported, for any pause or halt in this movement reveals the absence to which all modern magicians are subservient. Paralysis, the absence of movement, thus becomes the supreme danger in Jim's world. It is found in Jim's immobility on the deck of the *Patna* before he leaps from it; in the resemblance Jim bears to Billy Budd as he has difficulty speaking at passionate moments; in his fear that he may be buried alive as he struggles against the muddy riverbank in his escape from Rajah Allang; in his inability to deliver any last words; in Gentleman Brown's loathsomely similar narrative seizures; and in Marlow's own imitation of this condition in his storytelling: ". . . with the very first word uttered Marlow's body, extended at rest in the seat, would become very still." Paradoxically, that kind of stasis viewed as the end of desire thus comes to be the greatest threat towards the fulfillment of desire. Paralysis becomes the curse of Jim's imagination:

> "And you must remember he was a finished artist in that
> peculiar way, he was a gifted poor devil with the faculty of

swift and forestalling vision. The sights it showed him had
turned him into cold stone from the soles of his feet to the
nape of his neck; but there was a hot dance of thoughts in
his head, a dance of lame, blind, mute thoughts—a whirl
of awful cripples.''

While the imagination often appears in literature as the prey of
fabulous texts that seduce the reader into madness, crime, or sin, for
Jim—whose highest praise is " ' "They are like people in a book,
aren't they?" ' "—the imagination is dangerous precisely because it
fails to instruct or determine action. Instead, it opens man's consciousness to a range of significance that inhibits action because it so
overwhelms the limited and precise orders of social codes. As Jim's
imagination conceives of a purity that belonged to the adventure
narratives of his youth, to the cloistered thought of his father's study,
and, most profoundly, to the chivalrous traditions with which
Marlow compares Jim's relationship to Jewel, he is continually
threatened with paralysis because there is no room in the modern
world for this purity. Jim does not so much resemble Madame Bovary
or Frederick Moreau or even Don Quixote, then, as he does the
Hamlet who desires heroic sovereignty (a consideration indicated by
Stein's adaptation of the "To be or not to be" soliloquy to Jim's
case). In other words, Jim's problem is not just a misapprehension or
misapplication of romantic values but rather his paralyzing insistence
that these values not be compromised by any application short of
perfection. He would be a more conventional character if he believed
wrongly, but he is so fascinating to Marlow because he believes too
well. As the natives of Patusan take his metaphorical name for Jewel
and his own lordly self literally, so does Jim take literally the metaphors that the modern world can understand only in a figurative
sense. Thus he becomes, in effect, the scapegoat of a cultural change
that has taken place but that his civilization is still unprepared to
acknowledge openly.

Marlow argues against this dangerous imagination and for the
civilized function of repression:

"It's extraordinary how we go through life with eyes
half shut, with dull ears, with dormant thoughts. Perhaps
it's just as well; and it may be that it is this very dullness
that makes life to the incalculable majority so supportable
and so welcome.''

Ignorance, however, does not necessarily effectuate the control he desires. The closest representative in this novel to the triumphantly dull Captain McWhirr of Conrad's "Typhoon" is that Richard Cory figure, Captain Brierly; and the failure of his immaculate simplicity exemplifies the ultimate weakness of every other type of repression portrayed in the novel. And though his capacity for self-control might seem to be stronger than that of most people because it is subtler, Marlow himself comes to be haunted by the disorderly figures of Chester and Captain Robinson:

> "All at once, on the blank page, under the very point of the pen, the two figures of Chester and his antique partner, very distinct and complete, would dodge into view with stride and gestures, as if reproduced in the field of some optical toy. I would watch them for a while. No! They were too phantasmal and extravagant to enter into any one's fate. And a word carries far—very far—deals destruction through time as the bullets go flying through space."

As they represent " 'the blight of futility that lies in wait for men's speeches,' " that corruption of intention by which Marlow's offer of Patusan ends as hardly less squalid an opportunity than Chester's offer of a desert island smothered in guano, these figures undercut the repression by which Marlow seeks to maintain order in the world. However he may try to deny their reality in his world, he can no more succeed in doing so than he can in trying to deny his affinity with Jim.

For Marlow as for Jim, then, a continuous effort is necessary to preserve purity. Even if one possesses the alacrity of the youthful Stein, however, the end is in isolation, melancholy, and impotence. Imagination will out, and imagination is the ruination of desire because it is always prior to desire and therefore greater than any object to which desire may be directed. To the extent that Jim is typically "one of us"—and *Lord Jim* suggests that only such animalic figures as the captain of the *Patna* can do entirely without imagination—desire is always excessive in relation to its objects because imagination makes it belated in relation to those objects. However it may reach forward into the world, desire is always drawn back towards an imaginary past that alone could afford it full expression. It is in this sense that Jim's situation is virtually a parable of the situation of

desire in general, at least as this novel defines desire. His attempts to
be heroic are too late, as the novel suggests that all our attempts to
fulfill ourselves are too late, because no opportunity in the present
can measure up to the richness that has been offered by imagination
in the past. Thus it is that words deal destruction through time.
Whether they are picked up from boys' adventure stories or from
books of chivalry or from a dying Christianity, the conviction represented by Jim's situation—a conviction common to many writers
of Conrad's time—is that the modern world and modern man are
hostage to a past which they can neither return to nor turn away
from. The central psychological struggle of the modern world and of
modern man, according to this novel, lies in a desperate struggle to
overcome nostalgia. Jim is the naive representative of this problem;
Marlow, the worldly. Marlow, however, is as frustrated as Jim is in
his attempt to use an old rhetoric to meet the demands of a new
world.

It is imagination, then, that forces the knight to pause, and
consequently paralyzes him, as it forces him to confront the insuf-
ficiency of the world in relation to his desires. The crucial scenes in
Jim's life become emblematic of this condition:

> "The only distinct thought formed, vanishing, and re-
> forming in his brain, was: eight hundred people and seven
> boats; eight hundred people and seven boats."
>   . . . his mind positively flew round and round the serried
> circle of facts that had surged up all about him to cut him
> off from the rest of his kind: it was like a creature that,
> finding itself imprisoned within an enclosure of high stakes,
> dashes round and round, distracted in the night.

And even though Jim seems to escape from this kind of physical and
psychological imprisonment when he leaps over the fence of the
compound in Patusan and makes his way to the camp of Doramin,
all that he finally achieves is a colonial parody of his desire for self-
fulfillment, a parody that ends with his surrender to the influence of
Gentleman Brown.

IV

While Jim seeks to avoid the failure that the police court has attributed to him by projecting it onto a malevolent agency outside of

his control, Marlow seeks to prevent the superficial kinship he acknowledges between himself and Jim from taking on a more profound import by deploying his words with indirection and ambiguity. As Albert J. Guerard has written, *"Lord Jim* is as much a novel about a man who makes excuses as a novel that makes excuses." Rather than setting them free from an imprisoning world, however, the efforts of Marlow and Jim only result in a self-imprisoning paralysis or in an imprisoning relation to others. Marlow cannot help but be fascinated by Jim and trapped in his own words about Jim, while Jim is most captivated by Patusan when he seems most successful there. As Marlow comments upon Jim's relationship to Dain Waris,

> "I seemed to behold the very origin of friendship. If Jim took the lead, the other had captivated his leader. In fact, Jim the leader was a captive in every sense. The land, the people, the friendship, the love, were like the jealous guardians of his body. Every day added a link to the fetters of that strange freedom."

Such is the fate of the rule of lordship as, in a secular world, it becomes a profanity. Even where a magical freedom seems to appear, one can discern a more profound subjugation. This situation might be compared to that portrayed in Thomas Mann's "Mario and the Magician," in which the members of Cippola's audience are either paralyzed or made into automatons by virtue of the powerful magic through which "commanding and obeying formed together one single principle, one indissoluble unity . . . the one idea . . . comprehended in the other, as people and leader are comprehended in one another." Like the corrupting power that holds sway over Cippola's audience, such magical power as appears in the modern world of Conrad's novel will be exposed as having been drawn from a dark and malignant universe. A liberating and self-fulfilling magic is nowhere to be found, and it seems that the only possible response to such a situation is an uneasy repression, an intermittent and increasingly virulent paralysis, or utter passivity.

Thus it is that in recounting his reaction to Jim's story, Marlow says, " 'from his relation I am forced to believe he had preserved through it all a strange illusion of passiveness.' " He describes how Jim had partaken of this quality even in the act of narrating his tale: " 'He could no more stop telling now than he could have stopped living by the mere exertion of his will.' " This passivity—which is communicated to Marlow as he is " 'forced to believe' " Jim's attitude—eventuates in the magnificent banality of Marlow's cry to Jewel that " ' "nobody is good enough" ' " and in his equally empty cry to his auditors, " 'And what is the pursuit of truth, after all?' "

The real "plague spot" of Conrad's text is not its division between two locales but rather its disposition in the context of Christian heroism that makes Jim's experience in Patusan collapse into a semblance of his experience on the *Patna,* rendering him powerless and Marlow's words meaningless. The passivity that infects this text is the powerlessness of the ideal of heroism in the modern world that forces the desire for self-aggrandizement to end either in narcissistic torpor or in automatism, as in Jim's presentation of himself to be killed. The desires involved in "the call of an idea" that lures the pilgrims on the *Patna,* in Jim's "exquisite sensibility," and in Marlow's search " 'for a miracle' " all aim at a complete fulfillment of the self through the overcoming of history, but in the modern world of *Lord Jim* these desires can end only in the reduction of the subject to the status of an object. That magical state in which action would conform to its ideal cartography, where one could always find "the white streak of the wake drawn as straight by the ship's keel upon the sea as the black line drawn by the pencil upon the chart," is violated by the wounding of the *Patna,* by the " 'vein of subtle reference to their common blood' " that runs " 'through the rough talk' " between Jim and Gentleman Brown, by Jim's irremediable shame, and by Marlow's ultimate failure to come to terms with that shame—to find a rhetoric that would make sense of it instead of settling, as he does, for one that obscures it or deliberately casts off all pretensions to sense.

This situation does not change when one considers the love between Jim and Jewel even though Marlow says, as if it should make a difference, " 'Remember this is a love-story I am telling you now.' " This love is distinguished from all the other possibilites for desire in the novel—even from the superficially similar relationship between Stein and his late wife—because it is Jim's last chance. The servile version of this romance is that between Cornelius and Jewel's mother, while the potentially magic version is described by Marlow:

> "Our common fate . . . fastens upon the women with a peculiar cruelty. It does not punish like a master, but inflicts lingering torment, as if to gratify a secret, unappeas-

able spite. One would think that, appointed to rule on earth, it seeks to revenge itself upon the beings that come nearest to rising above the trammels of earthly caution; for it is only women who manage to put at times into their love an element just palpable enough to give one a fright— an extra-terrestrial touch. I ask myself with wonder—how the world can look to them—whether it has the shape and substance *we* know, the air *we* breathe! Sometimes I fancy it must be a region of unreasonable sublimities seething with the excitement of their adventurous souls, lighted by the glory of all possible risks and renunciations. However, I suspect there are very few women in the world, though of course I am aware of the multitudes of mankind and of the equality of the sexes in point of numbers—that is."

This third sex that transcends biological characteristics is the last hope for rehabilitation in the novel. Marlow would evade the difference between the world of modernity and that of myth by placing certain women both above and below men in their extreme capacity for both degradation and elevation. As a result, this third sex would unite both history and myth, duty and imagination, subjugation and liberation, and all the other contrarieties of this novel. (Jewel, after all, is half-white, half-native). Men would break free from those distances which this novel poses between male and female, East and West, narrator and subject and reader, and so on, to an identity secured within the thaumaturgic presence of such women, rare though they might be. This sex would overcome the bitter bond between truth and illusion otherwise enforced by the conditions of modern society. It would heal the wound of time that cuts through language and makes men liable to the pitiful misreadings dramatized by the survival of the *Patna* beyond the signs of its imminent demise, by Jim's misunderstanding of a reference to a dog as a reference to himself, and by Marlow's distrust of his auditors. One of the most banal of Victorian doctrines—that of the Angel in the House—is thus brought to a point of desperate complexity. Women save not because they are above men and superior to their world, but rather because they suffer more than men and through their suffering reflect back to men their imaginative selves. Women would be both men and not-men: apparently of the world of men, but through their superior suffering representing to men the superior world of the imagination to which they would belong if they could. To put Marlow's idea succinctly: Jim wants Jewel to be himself.

The condition of narcissism, which Freud related to magical practice, is thus specified once again as a central concern of this novel. Not only is this condition characteristic of Marlow's speech in its self-centered involutions, but he describes it as an aspect of Jim's speech—" 'He was not speaking to me, he was only speaking before me, in a dispute with an invisible personality, an antagonistic and inseparable partner of his existence—another possessor of his soul' "—and finds it reproduced in Jim's relationship with Jewel:

> "She lived so completely in his contemplation that she had acquired something of his outward aspect, something that recalled him in her movements, in the way she stretched her arm, turned her head, directed her glances. Her vigilant affection had an intensity that made it almost perceptible to the senses; it seemed actually to exist in the ambient matter of space, to envelop him like a peculiar fragrance. . . ."

> "Their soft murmurs reached me, penetrating, tender. . . . like a self-communion of one being carried on in two tones."

But Marlow's hypothesis of feminine salvation, despite its complex interpretation of the process of idealization, proves as ineffectual as every other possibility of rescue proposed in this novel. Although Jewel and Jim " 'came together under the shadow of a life's disaster, like knight and maiden meeting to exchange vows amongst haunted ruins,' " the haunting spirit of that disaster makes a travesty of their mutual pledges. Rather than saving Jim, Jewel's suffering remains a private matter that she can no more communicate to him than he can communicate to her the reason why he cannot leave Patusan. Their love only exacerbates his failure, expanding its scope, while Marlow's mythical idea of Jewel—like the natives'—only serves to emphasize all the more strongly the death of myth and the deathly power of its haunting memory.

V

Through his anti-eschatological narrative doctrine, Marlow resists the impression that Jim has made upon him:

"Are not our lives too short for that full utterance which through all our stammerings is of course our only and abiding intention? I have given up expecting those last words, whose ring, if they could only be pronounced, would shake both heaven and earth. There is never time to say our last word—the last word of our love, of our desire, faith, remorse, submission, revolt. . . . Frankly, it is not my words that I mistrust but your minds. I could be eloquent were I not afraid you fellows had starved your imaginations to feed your bodies."

This is the finest paradox of the novel: that Marlow, who begins with the desire to reveal Jim to his listeners and to himself, finally can do so only by deliberately rejecting the idea of revelation. Moreover, by going on to blame his disclaimer of revelation upon his relation to his audience rather than his relation to his own words, he shows himself as being essentially similar to Jim—who also is unable to convey any last words to the uncomprehending world—even as he seems to differentiate himself from Jim by refusing to seek some kind of magical materialization of meaning. Marlow, too, is forced by his narcissism to flee the world. Here, perhaps, in this epistemological complexity which suggests that the text of *Lord Jim* is situated at a point equally mystifying to its primary narrator, its characters, and its audience, is as good a locus as any to choose as a symbol of the modern departure in literature.

A further refinement of this irony is connected to the privilege of Marlow's final reader, a racist and conservative moralist of imperialism. His privilege derives, Marlow says, from the fact that only he showed " 'an interest . . . that survived the telling' " of Jim's story. His privilege is that of one who can resist Jim's baffling image, who can argue " 'that we must fight in the ranks or our lives don't count' " and who can find Jim wanting on that score whereas Marlow finally says, " 'I affirm nothing.' " In other words, he appears fit to receive the ending to Jim's tale precisely because he is so different from Jim—and yet he is not so. His imperial morality is Jim's narcissism on the scale of modern civilization. Though he has seemed to condemn Jim, in reality the ethos for which he stands ratifies in every respect the implications of Jim's anachronistic ideal. The real significance of the narcissistic, magical imagination of *Tuan* Jim is in the desire to dominate others totally. Self-fulfillment can mean nothing else if it is taken on the scale of ideal purity that Jim assumes as his own, for it is only through command over others that one could possibly see materially displayed the command over himself that Jim seeks. Paradoxically, then—and prophetically—this figure who seems so out of place is in reality the very image of Western imperialism in the modern world, the symptomatic incarnation of its demonic obsessiveness, its rhetorical emptiness, and its suicidal pridefulness. The parable of modern imperialism is written in this paradox: in the self-destructiveness of self-adoration.

Chronology

1857   Józef Teodor Konrad Korzeniowski born December 3, in Berdyczew, Poland, to Apollo Korzeniowski and Ewelina Bobrowska.

1862   Apollo Korzeniowski is exiled to Russia for his part in the Polish National Committee. His wife and son accompany him.

1865   Conrad's mother dies.

1869   Apollo Korzeniowski and son return to Cracow in February. Apollo dies on May 23.

1874   Conrad leaves Cracow for Marseilles, intending to become a sailor.

1875   Conrad is an apprentice aboard the *Mont Blanc,* bound for Martinique.

1877   Conrad is part owner of the *Tremolino,* which carries illegal arms to the Spanish pretender, Don Carlos.

1878   In February, after ending an unhappy love affair, Conrad attempts suicide by shooting himself. In June, he lands in England. He serves as ordinary seaman on the *Mavis.*

1883   Becomes mate on the ship *Riversdale.*

1884   Is second mate on the *Narcissus,* bound from Bombay to Dunkirk.

1886   Conrad becomes a naturalized British citizen.

1887   Is first mate on the *Highland Forest.*

1889   Begins writing *Almayer's Folly.*

1890   In May, Conrad leaves for the Congo as second in command of the S.S. *Roi de Belges,* later becoming commander.

1894   On January 14, he ends his sea career.

1895   Publishes *Almayer's Folly.* Writes *An Outcast of the Islands.* He is now living in London.

1896	Conrad marries Jessie George on March 24.
1897–1900	Writes *The Nigger of the "Narcissus," Heart of Darkness,* and *Lord Jim.*
1904	Completes *Nostromo.*
1905	Granted Civil List Pension. Travels in Europe for four months.
1907	Publishes *The Secret Agent.*
1911–12	Publishes *Under Western Eyes* and *'Twixt Land and Sea.*
1913	Publishes *Chance.*
1914	Writes *Victory.* Conrad visits Poland in July, where he is caught when the Great War breaks out on August 4. He escapes and returns safely to England in November.
1916	Conrad's son, Borys, is fighting on the French front.
1917	Publishes *The Shadow-Line* and prefaces to an edition of his collected works.
1918	Armistice, November 11.
1919	Conrad publishes *The Arrow of Gold.* He moves to Oswalds, Bishopsbourne, near Canterbury, where he spends his last years.
1920	Publishes *The Rescue.*
1924	In May, Conrad declines a knighthood. After an illness, he dies of a heart attack on August 3. He is buried in Canterbury.
1925	The incomplete *Suspense* published. *Tales of Hearsay* published.
1926	*Last Essays* published.

Contributors

HAROLD BLOOM, Sterling Professor of the Humanities at Yale University, is the author of *The Anxiety of Influence, Poetry and Repression,* and many other volumes of literary criticism. His forthcoming study, *Freud: Transference and Authority,* attempts a full-scale reading of all of Freud's major writings. A MacArthur Prize Fellow, he is general editor of five series of literary criticism published by Chelsea House. During 1987–88, he was appointed Charles Eliot Norton Professor of Poetry at Harvard University.

ELLIOTT B. GOSE, JR., is Professor of English at the University of British Columbia. He is the author of *Imagination Indulged: The Irrational in the Nineteenth-Century Novel.*

PETER J. GLASSMAN is Associate Professor of English at Tulane University. He is the author of *Language and Being: Joseph Conrad and the Literature of Personality.*

D. M. HALPERIN is Assistant Professor of Literature in the Department of Humanities at M.I.T. He is the author of *Before Pastoral: Theocritus and the Ancient Tradition of Bucolic Poetry.*

IAN WATT is Professor of English at Stanford University. His books include *The Rise of the Novel, Conrad in the Nineteenth Century,* and the forthcoming *Gothic and Comic: Two Variations on the Realistic Tradition.*

SURESH RAVAL is Associate Professor of English at the University of Arizona. He is the author of *Metacriticism.*

J. HILLIS MILLER is Professor of English at the University of California, Irvine. His books include *Charles Dickens: The World of His Novels, Poets of Reality,* and *The Form of Victorian Fiction.*

Daniel Cottom is Assistant Professor of English at Wayne State University. He has published on Defoe, George Eliot, Hawthorne and Melville.

Bibliography

Bender, Todd K., R. J. Dilligan, and James W. Parins, eds. *A Concordance to Conrad's* Lord Jim. New York and London: Garland Publishing, 1976.

Berman, Jeffrey. *Joseph Conrad: Writing as Rescue.* New York: Astra Books, 1977.

Berthoud, Jacques. *Joseph Conrad: The Major Phase.* Cambridge: Cambridge University Press, 1978.

Bruss, Paul S. "Marlow's Interview with Stein: The Implication of the Metaphor." *Studies in the Novel* 5 (1973): 491–503.

Burstein, Janet. "On Ways of Knowing *Lord Jim.*" *Nineteenth-Century Fiction* 26 (1972): 456–68.

Conradiana: A Journal of Joseph Conrad Studies, 1968–.

Cox, C. B. "The Metamorphosis of Lord Jim." *The Critical Quarterly* 15, no. 1 (1973): 9–31.

Crankshaw, Edward. *Joseph Conrad: Some Aspects of the Novel.* New York: Russell & Russell, 1963.

Daleski, H. M. *Joseph Conrad: The Way of Dispossession.* London: Faber & Faber, 1977.

Ehrsam, R. G. *A Bibliography of Joseph Conrad.* Metuchen, N J : Scarecrow, 1969.

Epstein, Harry S. "*Lord Jim* as a Tragic Action." *Studies in the Novel* 5 (1973): 229–47.

Garnett, Edward. *Letters from Joseph Conrad, 1895–1924.* Indianapolis: Bobbs-Merrill, 1928.

Gekoski, R. A. *Conrad: The Moral World of the Novelist.* New York: Harper & Row, 1978.

Gillon, Adam. *The Eternal Solitary.* New York: Bookman, 1960.

———. *Joseph Conrad.* Boston: Twayne, 1982.

Gillon, Adam and Ludwik Krzyzanowski, eds. *Joseph Conrad: Commemorative Essays.* New York: Astra Books, 1975.

Gose, Elliott B., Jr. "Pure Exercise of Imagination: Archetypal Symbolism in *Lord Jim.*" *PMLA* 79 (1964): 137–47.

Guerard, Albert J. *Conrad the Novelist.* Cambridge: Harvard University Press, 1958.

———. *Joseph Conrad.* New York: New Directions, 1947.

Haugh, Robert F. "The Structure of *Lord Jim.*" *College English* 13 (1951): 137–41.

Hawthorn, Jeremy. *Joseph Conrad.* London: E. Arnold, 1979.

Johnson, Bruce M. "Conrad's 'Karain' and *Lord Jim.*" *Modern Language Quarterly* 26 (1963): 13–20.

Joseph Conrad Today: The Newsletter of the Joseph Conrad Society of America, 1975–.

Karl, Frederick R. *A Reader's Guide to Joseph Conrad.* Rev. ed. New York: Noonday Press, 1969.

————, ed. *Joseph Conrad: A Collection of Criticism.* New York: McGraw-Hill, 1975.

Kirschner, Paul. *Conrad: The Psychologist as Artist.* Edinburgh: Oliver & Boyd, 1968.

Kramer, Dale. "Marlow, Myth, and Structure in *Lord Jim.*" *Criticism* 8 (1966): 263–79.

Kuehn, Robert E. *Twentieth Century Interpretations of* Lord Jim: *A Collection of Critical Essays.* Englewood Cliffs, N.J.: Prentice-Hall, 1969.

La Bossière, Camille R. *Joseph Conrad and the Science of Unknowing.* Fredericton, N.B., Canada: York Press, 1979.

Leavis, F. R. *The Great Tradition.* London: Chatto & Windus, 1948.

Malbone, Raymond Gates. " 'How to Be': Marlow's Quest in *Lord Jim.*" *Twentieth Century Literature* 10 (1965): 172–80.

Morf, Gustav. *The Polish Heritage of Joseph Conrad.* London: Haskell, 1930.

Moser, Thomas, ed. *Joseph Conrad:* Lord Jim. A Norton Critical Edition. New York: Norton, 1968.

Nettels, Elsa. *James and Conrad.* Athens: University of Georgia Press, 1977.

Newell, Kenneth B. "The Yellow Dog Incident in Conrad's *Lord Jim.*" *Studies in the Novel* 3 (1971): 26–33.

Palmer, John A. *Joseph Conrad's Fiction: A Study in Literary Growth.* Ithaca, N.Y.: Cornell University Press, 1968.

Roussel, Royal. *The Metaphysics of Darkness: A Study in the Unity of Conrad's Fiction.* Baltimore: The Johns Hopkins University Press, 1971.

Said, Edward W. *Beginnings: Intention and Method.* New York: Basic Books, 1975.

————. *Joseph Conrad and the Fiction of Autobiography.* Cambridge: Harvard University Press, 1966.

Schwarz, Daniel R. "The Journey to Patusan: The Education of Jim and Marlow in Conrad's *Lord Jim.*" *Studies in the Novel* 4 (1972): 442–58.

Sherry, Norman. *Conrad's Eastern World.* Cambridge: Cambridge University Press, 1966.

————, ed. *Conrad: The Critical Heritage.* London: Routledge & Kegan Paul, 1973.

————, ed. *Joseph Conrad: A Commemoration.* New York: Harper & Row, 1977.

Tanner, Tony. "Butterflies and Beetles—Conrad's Two Truths." *Chicago Review* 16, no. 1 (1963): 123–40.

————, ed. *Conrad:* Lord Jim. Great Neck, N.Y.: Barron's Educational Series, 1963.

Tenenbaum, Elizabeth B. " 'And the Woman is Dead Now': A Reconsideration of Conrad's Stein." *Studies in the Novel* 10 (1978): 335–45.

Tennant, Roger. *Joseph Conrad: A Biography.* New York: Atheneum, 1981.

Thornburn, David. *Conrad's Romanticism.* New Haven: Yale University Press, 1974.

Van Ghent, Dorothy. *The English Novel: Form and Function.* New York: Harper & Brothers, 1961.

Verleun, Jan. *"Patna" and Patusan Perspectives.* Groningen, The Netherlands: Bouma, 1979.

Watt, Ian. *Conrad in the Nineteenth Century.* Berkeley and Los Angeles: University of California Press, 1979.

Weinstein, Philip M. *The Semantics of Desire: Changing Models of Identity from Dickens to Joyce*. Princeton: Princeton University Press, 1984.

Whitehead, Lee M. "Recent Conrad Criticism." *Dalhousie Review* 61, no. 4 (1981–82): 743–49.

Wiley, Paul L. *Conrad's Measure of Man*. New York: Gordian Press, 1966.

Yelton, D. C. *Mimesis and Metaphor: An Inquiry into the Genesis and Scope of Conrad's Symbolic Imagery*. The Hague: Mouton, 1967.

Zabel, Morton Dauwen. *Craft and Character in Modern Fiction*. New York: Viking, 1957.

Zyla, W. T., and W. M. Aycock, eds. *Joseph Conrad: Theory and World Fiction*. Lubbock: Texas Tech University, 1974.

Acknowledgments

"The Truth in the Well" (originally entitled "*Lord Jim*") by Elliot B. Gose, Jr., from *Imagination Indulged: The Irrational in the Nineteenth-Century Novel* by Elliot B. Gose Jr., © 1972 by McGill-Queen's University Press. Reprinted by permission of the publisher.

"An Intelligible Picture: *Lord Jim*" by Peter J. Glassman from *Language and Being: Joseph Conrad and the Literature of Personality* by Peter J. Glassman, © 1976 by Peter J. Glassman. Reprinted by permission.

"*Lord Jim* and the Pear Tree Caper" by D. M. Halperin from *American Notes and Queries* 14, no. 8 (April 1976). © 1976 by Erasmus Press. Reprinted by permission of the author and *American Notes and Queries*.

"The Ending" (originally entitled "*Lord Jim*") by Ian Watt from *Conrad in the Nineteenth Century* by Ian Watt, © 1979 by the Regents of the University of California. Reprinted by permission of the University of California Press.

"Narrative Authority in *Lord Jim*: Conrad's Art of Failure" by Suresh Raval from *ELH* 48, no. 2 (Summer 1981), © 1981 by the Johns Hopkins University Press, Baltimore/London. Reprinted by permission of the Johns Hopkins University Press.

"*Lord Jim*: Repetition as Subversion of Organic Form" by J. Hillis Miller from *Fiction and Repetition: Seven English Novels* by J. Hillis Miller, © 1982 by the President and Fellows of Harvard College. Reprinted by permission of Harvard University Press.

"*Lord Jim*: Destruction through Time" by Daniel Cottom from *The Centennial Review* 27, no. 1 (Winter 1983), © 1983 by *The Centennial Review*. Reprinted by permission.

Index